IGNITING WRITERS
PROPELLING AUTHORS

LAUNCHING YOU

SHERRY WARD

SQUARE TREE PUBLISHING
www.SquareTreePublishing.com

Copyright © 2024 by Sherry Ward

All rights reserved, including the right of reproduction in whole or in part in any form. No part of this book may be reproduced or used in any manner without written permission of the copyright owner. For permission requests, please contact the copyright holder at info@squaretreepublishing.com.

Scripture quotations marked NIV are taken from the Holy Bible, New International Version®, NIV®. Copyright © 1973, 1978, 1984, 2011 by Biblica, Inc.TM Used by permission of www.Zondervan.com All rights reserved worldwide. The "NIV" and "New International Version" are trademarks registered in the United States Patent and Trademark Office by Biblica, Inc.TM

Scripture quotations marked (NLT) are taken from the Holy Bible, New Living Translation, copyright ©1996, 2004, 2015 by Tyndale House Foundation. Used by permission of Tyndale House Publishers, Carol Stream, Illinois 60188. All rights reserved.

For more information about bulk purchases, please contact Square Tree Publishing at info@squaretreepublishing.com. The author may earn commissions from affiliate links at no extra cost to you, helping to support the content provided.

Cover design by Sharon Marta

Paperback: ISBN 978-1-957293-56-1
Hardcover: ISBN 978-1-957293-60-8

Library of Congress Control Number: 2024925861

DEDICATION

I dedicate this book to all the Square Tree authors who gave God their YES, *despite* their circumstances. You pressed through challenges like Nehemiah, with one hand on the work and the other on your weapon, to complete the book God called you to write.

God has launched you in unexpected ways, some to the heights of the United Nations, governmental legislature, media, and others to international ministries. So many Square Tree authors have launched in countless ways, whose stories, if told, would fill this book and so many more (John 21:25).

For those still on the launchpad as you write your book, may God give you opportunities beyond your wildest dreams, as you work through the healing and complete your book. I am forever grateful to be a part of what God has planned for you as He propels you into your destiny.

FOREWORD

You don't realize how hard it is to write a book until you try. As someone who is still deep in the dark night of the soul while writing my memoir, Sherry's voice and wisdom has been a light shining the way through writing some of the hardest stories of my life. She's spent hours (sometimes late into the night) helping me unpack what's happening during the writing process. And now she's bringing that wisdom to the scores of soon-to-be authors that God has called.

Launching You is a book that takes you beyond the mechanics of publishing, into the heart of the matter of what happens when an author sits down to write. Sherry offers a heartfelt invitation to embrace your mission, refine your message, and share your story with the world. Sherry brings together sharp, practical strategies and a deep understanding of the heart behind writing, offering not just guidance on the mechanics but also the courage and mindset needed to take that bold step into the world. Her experience, both personal and professional, makes every chapter a well of wisdom and inspiration.

What makes this book special is how deeply Sherry understands the journey. Writing a book isn't just about words on a page; it's about transformation for the author and for the people who read

LAUNCHING YOU

it. Through this process, you'll learn to trust God's timing, navigate challenges, and discover the joy of sharing your story in a way that impacts lives—including your own.

I met Sherry back in 2021 when she hired me for marketing support, and I remember the first time she attended one of my events—she seemed quite shy and reserved. At this particular event, we were doing a team-building competition that required groups of 8-10 to go on a scavenger hunt all throughout Disney World. Sherry, the quiet one in the group, surprised everyone. She became the team's secret weapon, scouring every corner with relentless focus. Thanks to her determination, her team claimed victory. That moment wasn't just fun—it revealed Sherry's unwavering grit, attention to detail, and drive to see things through. Those are the exact qualities she brings to her authors and now to you, the reader.

Working with Sherry has been one of the most rewarding experiences of my career. As a coach and well-versed marketer, I've had the privilege of guiding many extraordinary individuals, but Sherry's transformation stands out.

She is the kind of person you want in your corner when embarking on a journey as challenging and transformative as writing a book. Her passion is infectious, her guidance practical, and her ability to unlock potential unmatched—like the time she stayed up with me until nearly midnight, helping me organize my writing so I could share hard stories without hurting people I love. Her eye for detail and knack for asking the right questions brought clarity I didn't even know I needed. Whether you're writing to heal, launch a ministry, or expand your business, Sherry's unique approach ensures you don't just complete a book—you step into a calling.

FORWARD

Sherry, thank you for allowing me to witness your journey and for letting me play a small part in your incredible story. To the reader: this book is more than a resource—it's your partner in a journey of growth, healing, and impact. As you turn these pages, let Sherry's wisdom and passion guide you toward a launch that changes not just your life, but the lives of those you're called to reach.

With admiration and gratitude,
Julie Chenell
Co-founder of Funnel Gorgeous® & Founder of Digital Insiders

TABLE OF CONTENTS

INTRODUCTION
Prepare for Liftoff 11

PREPARING TO LAUNCH
Chapter 1 – The Gravity of "WHY" 17
Chapter 2 – The "WHO" Behind Your Mission 31
Chapter 3 – Navigating Genres 43
Chapter 4 – Writing for Healing 55
Chapter 5 – Shifting Mindset Blocks 69

LAUNCHING YOU
Chapter 6 – Mission "Ministry" 87
Chapter 7 – Rocketing Your Business 97
Chapter 8 – Throttle up as a Professional Author 111
Chapter 9 – Satellite Speaker 121

LAUNCHING BEYOND
Chapter 10 – Navigating the Marketing Milky Way 135
Chapter 11 – Community Launchpad 147
Chapter 12 – Launching a Movement 159
Conclusion – Reentry 167
Not Your Typical Epilogue – It's Not About You! 175

Introduction
PREPARE FOR LIFTOFF

The air was silenced, as if every molecule was frozen in time, as my coworkers and I helplessly watched the explosive fireball. What had begun as our most triumphant moment vaporized everything in an instant.

I was a sixteen-year-old intern at Rockwell International working on the Space Shuttle Challenger in Southern California. My department, Logistics, was the parts division of the company. Our desks were housed in an airplane hangar the size of the International Space Station, retrofitted into chest-high cubicles so you could see everyone around you.

By the 1980s, the popularity of space travel was waning. NASA wanted to highlight its importance to everyday, ordinary people, so on this mission, they decided to put the first civilian in flight, a social studies teacher from New Hampshire named Christa McAuliffe. McAuliffe was a gifted communicator set to teach two lessons on the spacecraft: "The Ultimate Field Trip" and "Where We've Been, Where We're Going."

On January 28, 1986, the company brought in big screen TVs so we could watch the launch. Years of our work had culminated into a single day...a single launch.

The excitement around the room was electric as colleagues

LAUNCHING YOU

completed last-minute tasks before witnessing this amazing feat of human accomplishment.

I stood there that fateful day, cheering and high-fiving co-workers as the Challenger lifted off.

Seventy-three seconds. That was it...less than it takes to send an email. Seventy-three seconds after takeoff, the Challenger exploded.

A day etched forever into my memory. I stood dumbfounded. Intense emotions—much like those we all felt during the September 11th terrorist attacks— overwhelmed me, yet this horrific accident was something I was part of.

It was determined later that a faulty O-ring was the cause of the accident. This ignored O-ring had played a critical role. Compromised in the cold weather, NASA managers disregarded engineers who warned them of a potential impending disaster.

One small, seemingly insignificant part, one terribly cold night, one poorly timed launch, destroyed the mission and all life on board the shuttle.

Had the temperature risen, things would have been different.

The shuttle was simply launched at the wrong time.

****

God has a mission for you. He is preparing to launch you, and the smallest details of your life, those that may seem inconsequential to you, He is concerned about. He knows if He moves too soon or during the wrong conditions, you may blow up—self-destruct like the *Challenger* did.

Waiting may be difficult; you groan and complain because completing your book seems to take forever. But He's working

INTRODUCTION

behind the scenes to make sure your spiritual O-rings are securely fastened for the ride He's about to take you on.

You are reading this book right now for a reason.

God has gifted "ordinary people" to bring His revelation from Heaven to Earth. You may not be a professional writer yet, but you are part of the motley crowd God is going to use to change the world.

Like King David's mighty men who became disenfranchised with the world's systems—in debt and rejected—it is this exact group of people God desires to use to change atmospheres and shift nations: courageous individuals who may not be as polished and professional (yet), but who will usher His Kingdom into this world to people who desperately need it.

And it starts with YOU!

God is about to take you on the *"Ultimate Field Trip"* to show you *"Where you have been, and where you're going."*

So don't despise the days of small beginnings. God is at work in this refining season of your life. He wants you fully healed so you'll heal others, restore families, build finances, and repair relationships. He desires to strengthen those weak O-rings inside of you so you can soar into His atmosphere with a message of hope to those you're called to reach.

Although there is no magic formula for launching a person, there are some commonalities that all successful authors, especially at Square Tree Publishing, have that are outlined in this book. Practical and powerful insights to ensure you are prepared and launched at the proper time.

This book is divided into three main parts. The first section, *Preparing to Launch,* helps you focus on WHY you are writing your book and WHO you are writing it for; including how to select

LAUNCHING YOU

your specific genre, discover healing through your writing, and overcome any mindset blocks you may have as a writer.

The *Launching You* section helps you determine HOW your book will propel you—whether as a speaker, professional author, ministry leader, or by starting or growing a business.

Launch Beyond covers marketing strategies, the importance of community, and how to start a movement. Each section builds on the previous one, empowering you to launch in ways you never imagined—impacting your business, ministry, or family.

It is my hope and prayer that this book launches an entire community of writers—authors who will champion wild, unorthodox feats of faith, which will be a sign and wonder of God's power here on Earth.

Place your seats in the upright position and your tray tables up, because God is getting ready to LAUNCH YOU!

PREPARING TO LAUNCH

CHAPTER 1
THE GRAVITY OF "WHY"

In 2017, the National Aeronautics and Space Administration (NASA) turned its attention back to the Moon—something it hadn't done since 1972—by initiating the Artemis Program. This time, with the intention of reestablishing a human presence and the goal of creating a permanent base to facilitate human missions to Mars and, essentially, to "go where no man has gone before." While the mission of Apollo 11 was to get the first man to the Moon, the next phase of space travel is leveraging the Moon to get to Mars, with the Moon serving as a gateway to reach higher levels in the heavens.

****

This is exactly God's intent for you: to be launched into higher places that He has prepared for you, and your book is the gateway in which He'll do this. The directors of the Artemis Program needed to know the WHY—why they were investing the time, technology, money, and workforce to go to the Moon on a more permanent basis. It had to be a far greater "why" than the first trip (which was a huge accomplishment for that era).

You also need to know WHY you are writing your book. It's the first critical step before liftoff. It is imperative that your why is crystal clear from the beginning. It will guide not only the structure of your book, but

LAUNCHING YOU

how you will market it, too. You may not yet know all the details of your how, but you must know why you are writing your book.

Wrong Reasons for Writing Your Book

"Wow, you have an incredible story of overcoming adversity. You should write a book," well-meaning people may have said to you.

You may have an incredible story of healing from trauma, triumphing over compelling circumstances, even surviving the worst, yet that may not be enough to face the work it takes to write a book and the spiritual warfare that ensues.

You have a good story to tell of redemption, but has God told you to write it? Have you asked Him? Is He really calling you to pen this story, or are there other ways He wants your message to be shared? Giving your testimony to a small home church group is powerful and shouldn't be underestimated. There are many ways to share your story other than writing a book. Although friends and family have told you, "It'll be a bestseller, for sure," you must do it ONLY if God is calling you to do so.

"But I've gone through so much trauma, surely it can't all be in vain?" God guarantees in His word that it is never in vain, but if you are using your book as some sort of redemptive tool to make sense of all the crazy trauma you've been through, in the false belief that writing the book will somehow make sense of the senseless abuse, this is the wrong "why" and will lead to disappointment and disillusionment. You may be thinking this on an unconscious level, not realizing it. This is especially true for those who are writing memoirs. Please pray and ask God to reveal His direction, His WHY.

The benchmark question to ask yourself is, *"Is this the book I am meant to write, or is it just me trying to redeem the bad things that have happened in my life?"*

THE GRAVITY OF "WHY"

Perhaps you're a fiction writer, and an idea came to you in a dream or as a random thought. You're super creative, and interesting scenarios come to you all the time. Which one is the God-idea, and which one is just from your imagination? Maybe you told people about your idea, and they got excited and said, "You should write a book!" Whatever genre you may write in, the WHY will always be the foundation to where God will take you.

"God, is this the idea you want me to fully develop into a book?" This is the question you must ask yourself, first and foremost.

Now, this is not meant to discourage you but to lead you to focus on what God is calling you to do. What I am not saying is, are you talented enough? Are you creative enough? Moses felt he was unqualified to speak, and even jumped out ahead of God to lead the Israelites. God had indeed called him, yet the time and opportunity came at God's choosing, not his.

I've Written the Story, Now What?

Once you've asked God if you're to write your story, the second question is, "Am I supposed to *publish* my story?"

This may seem counterintuitive. "If God wants me to write my story, then surely He wants me to publish it?" But this isn't always the case. Often God gives us assignments that don't always seem to make sense, like writing the book but not publishing it.

One of our Square Tree authors went through tremendous sexual abuse as a young man and began to write his story. As he finished the manuscript, he felt God tell him, "Don't publish your story." There were people still alive in his life that had caused the offense, and he felt it was not time to publish his manuscript. However, there was tremendous healing that happened as he wrote his story. God showed up in huge ways to restore him from the past and bring forgiveness to the perpetrators in his life. He's since gone on

LAUNCHING YOU

to write a second book that he does feel called to publish. So, the first book he wrote and *didn't* publish paved the way to his healing journey to write the second book, which he *did* feel led to publish.

As you write, especially if it is your memoir, the simple act of writing your story can bring the healing God wants to offer you. It was never about the book; it was about God using the writing to help you heal. The *healing comes through the writing*. So, write, but as you do, be open to the WHY that He has for you.

Healing is the primary goal God has for you, but additionally, He may want to align you, properly positioning you for the next thing He has planned.

Once you know conclusively God has called you to write and publish your story, there are endless ways that God may launch you, but let's discuss the four most common scenarios. These scenarios are for both nonfiction and fiction authors. Read through them all and ask God which one He may be doing in your life. Be open, however, because you may not know which one until *after* you write and publish your book!

Launching You in a Different Direction

THE GRAVITY OF "WHY"

"I don't recognize myself anymore! I'm not the same person I was a year ago before being in the Square Tree community and working with Dr. Amanda, the Square Tree Cognitive Release Coach. She has helped me to find my voice," Irene exclaimed.

Launching you in a new direction will require you to find healing through the trauma you have experienced. This scenario applies to **memoirs, Christian devotionals, and Christian Living genres.**

Do you want to write a memoir?

Memoir authors often write about the tremendous amount of trauma, abuse, or life-altering experiences they have gone through.

Does this describe your life?

God uses memoirs as a vehicle of restoration. Of course, this kind of book isn't written in a month or two but is a slow progression of processing the hurt and pain while writing. It's about finding your voice and coming out of those hidden dark places that have kept you bound for years.

When finished, a true inner healing is found that could have only come through writing the book. God may want this book to be published, to go out to friends, family, and to those who may have suffered the same sort of abuse, to release encouragement and give an opportunity for family members to find redemption as well because of the brave vulnerability of bringing things long hidden to the forefront.

Writing and publishing this book may never have been about selling tons of copies but about finding healing and, afterwards, launching the author in a completely different direction, perhaps having nothing to do with the topic of the book.

Psychologist Dr. Evelin Garcia wrote her first book as a tribute to her mom, who, as a single mother with young girls, immigrated from El Salvador to the U.S., and who had recently passed away. Dr. Garcia's

LAUNCHING YOU

book *Mamá Decía (Mother Says)* recounts the top ten lessons her mother taught her while growing up. This book helped Evelin heal from the loss of her mother. It was not about book sales but about leaving a legacy and a tribute to her mom. This book did help others, but it brought the healing she needed to write her next book, *Doctora Decía (Doctor Says)*, which addressed the topic of forgiveness. It was her second book that launched her as a speaker before influential organizations, such as the United Nations, national government organizations, and universities. The first book paved the way for the second one, which launched *her*.

This may be hard to understand or accept. "You mean, I may be doing something completely different from what I think I am called to do?" Remember, healing is never a consolation prize but is necessary for the next chapter He has for you. Be yielded to God's plan. An author who resists may continue to market their book, not wanting to feel publishing it was in vain, yet misses the true power of the healing that is taking place. If they only knew the amazing new door God is about to open for them—one that would never have been available to them if they hadn't written the book—then they would feel an excitement for what God wants to do next!

Square Tree author Jessica Baker wrote her memoir *Unbecoming*, which released tremendous healing in her, but she never imagined the doors that would open after writing her book. Jessica joined our Square Tree team at a professional businesswomen conference in Florida. During that conference, I told the women that it was critical to hire a prayer intercessory team because just having friends to pray for them intermittently wasn't fully covering them or their business. At the end, I said, "If you want my prayer team to pray for you, let us know." Jessica is one of our intercessors at Square Tree, and little did I know that this one unplanned statement would open the floodgates of women who came up asking for prayer. She soon lost count of the number of people

THE GRAVITY OF "WHY"

she prayed over! At the end of the conference, someone approached her and asked if she would be a paid intercessor for their company. Writing the book, gaining healing, and finding her voice were all preparation for God to take Jessica into a totally new direction she didn't see coming. It was amazing to have a front-row seat to God launching Jessica. The excitement and awe she experienced made all the hard work of writing the book totally worth it.

It is shortsighted to simply want your book to soar to number one on the New York Times Best Seller list and become a movie. Expand your vision to see how God may be using your book to launch you into something tremendously better and *completely life-changing*. This amazing new direction may have never come into view except for writing the book. Do you feel this resonates inside? An excited nervousness or that feeling of, "Oh, Lord, I think this is me!" If you feel this scenario is you, don't despise the days of small beginnings. God needs to heal you BEFORE He can launch you. Stay the course and watch the amazing new direction God will lead you into.

Launching You in Ministry

LAUNCHING YOU

"I want to start a ministry to help moms who have young adult children addicted to drugs," Cathy Taylor said at our lunch meeting.

Cathy Taylor knew the heartache of watching her daughter struggle with drug addiction and become out of control. She did everything she knew to do, yet felt frustrated and alone. She wanted to write a book and curriculum specifically to help mothers cope with their addicted children's self-destructive behaviors and find healthy ways to manage the emotional pain it caused. Her memoir and curriculum were in direct alignment with the ministry she birthed. Cathy was already teaching classes at her local church from material she had written in a three-ring notebook, but the team at Square Tree worked with her to officially launch the Hurting Moms, Mending Hearts ministry all over the U.S. and Canada.

Is your goal to launch a ministry through your book?

Launching into a new ministry will require a good deal of healing before ministering effectively to others. This scenario applies to the **memoirs, Christian devotionals, and Christian Living genres.**

Cathy found a measure of healing, even reconciling with her daughter as she led her small home church ministry. She developed her curriculum, shared her testimony at events, and eventually wrote her memoir. Authors like Cathy have been through trauma, still feel the pain, but unlike the first scenario, the message they carry is the *same as the audience they'll serve in their ministry.*

For example, if you're a survivor of domestic violence, then your ministry would have the same focus, serving those who have gone through domestic violence. Your story of healing brings relatability and authenticity to your book. When someone picks it up, they feel you know exactly what they're going through.

In the first scenario, God seeks to bring healing, guiding you toward a new direction—one that wouldn't have been possible without the healing

THE GRAVITY OF "WHY"

that comes through writing your book. In the second scenario, God still wants you to find healing, but He is launching you into the same type of ministry as your book's theme. You'll still find your voice and come out of those hidden dark places, but the purpose is to go back to those same places and bring hope and healing to others. There may be multiple traumas you've experienced, so selecting one to be the focus of your story is vital.

You may be launched into an international ministry like Cathy's, or simply to your local church community. The extent of your reach is in God's hands and what He has placed in your heart, but it will make the intended impact He has planned for you.

As you develop your ministry, other needs may surface just beyond the scope of your purpose. As the leader, you might feel compelled to venture into those areas, to help *everyone*. Allow other ministries to be birthed through yours. For example, as Cathy was ministering to the hurting moms, some of them faced grief and loss at the death of their young adult children to drug abuse. These women needed more help. This led to the Grieving Moms, Mending Hearts ministry, with Jacke Van Woerkom (Rose), a grieving mom herself, at the helm. You may never fully realize the impact of your ministry or how it may inspire the birth of other amazing ministries.

Launching You as a Professional Author

LAUNCHING YOU

"I'm now writing a Manga (Japanese inspired graphic novel), in addition to my fifth book coming out," Joel Fisher, our Square Tree author excitedly shared.

Joel is a fantasy/religious fiction writer who has published several series of books. He tells the universal story of heroes and villains and the struggles they face.

God can use fictional tales to bring about the restoration He desires. Joel loved playing fantasy video games with his brother as a young boy. When his brother passed away suddenly, Joel was heartbroken. Some years later, he discovered some of his brother's writings. Joel felt God's tug to bring his brother's stories to life, and the book was used to bring healing to Joel over the death of his brother. Don't discount fiction bringing healing into your life. Many Square Tree fiction authors have similar testimonies.

Niching Down

The decision to write professionally, as Joel did, may require choosing one specific genre to settle into. This can open opportunities to create a book series, giving you a returning audience and allowing for the sale of a larger quantity of books. This will enable you to run paid ads that will be more cost-effective, which we will discuss later. The first book sets the tone from which the rest of the books will flow.

This Launch You scenario applies to the **fiction authors and serial nonfiction authors.**

A professional fictional series author is positioned for some fantastic opportunities. Many movies are based on book series. Square Tree Publishing and Productions has partnered with the Jack London Award-winning science fiction/fantasy writer Jonathan Yanez and Wolf Pack Entertainment to create a film version of his number one selling book,

THE GRAVITY OF "WHY"

Forsaken Mercenary. Jonathan's full sci-fi series includes twelve books, which is very appealing to Hollywood. If the first book is successful, it paves the way for book sales of the rest of the books, as well as a movie sequel.

When you write a book and copyright it, you own the intellectual property (IP) of the book. The advantage of writing a book from an intellectual property perspective is when your words are written and recorded, it is protected by copyright, preventing others from stealing and claiming it as their own. Producers and film distributors love this, for as the owner, you have exclusive rights, and they deal with you alone. It is one way to set you apart from all the rest of the people pitching their movie ideas in Hollywood.

Nonfiction works may not come to mind as an obvious book series, but it's possible. I have a three-book series revolving around the tough "Wilderness" season that Christians often go through: *Wilderness Season, Crossing the Jordan, and The Promised Land.* All of these books tie together in a theme, just like a fictional series would, within the niche area they are written. For both nonfiction and fiction authors, writing a series leads to an audience following. Narrowing down your audience and genre is essential if you wish to make a living from writing and generate significant book sales, which in turn may lead to speaking engagements.

When you find your niche and genre, generate a consistent and constant flow of new material. This is the habit Jonathan Yanez has developed, writing a book a month for years. He has penned over eighty books, creating much revenue potential as a professional author. However, he is the exception; yet the principle to "keep the books coming" is a solid one.

LAUNCHING YOU

Launching You in Business and as a Speaker

This Launch You scenario applies to authors who desire to launch a new or existing business and with any suitable type of genre that attracts quality leads falling within the business nonfiction category. Your book can build your authority so people will trust you and purchase your products or services.

Marlena Gross runs a home organization business and wrote a children's book entitled, *Ana Learns to Clean Her Room*. Within the book, there are checklists for parents to help teach their children how to clean their room systematically. She's building her authority for her business as a home organizer. This Launch You scenario applies to authors who desire to launch a new or existing business and with any suitable type of genre that attracts quality leads falling within the business nonfiction category. Your book can build your authority so people will trust you and purchase your products or services.

A book can bring quality leads to your existing business and build your authority in your sphere of influence. Dr. Jonathan Clark came to Square Tree Publishing after hearing me as a guest on Shawn Bolz's podcast, *Exploring the Market*. Dr. Clark is a Western medical doctor that loves holistic medicine. He published two books to build his authority

THE GRAVITY OF "WHY"

in the holistic medicine field and to attract other medical doctors to the new medical collective he was forming. The goal of the medical collective is to bring doctors together from all over the United States—Christian physicians and therapists working together and referring one another.

In addition to products, a book can launch a service-based business, such as personal coaching. Dr. Amanda Helman's book, *Silent No Longer,* launched her coaching career. Her subtitle, *Finding My Voice After Complex Trauma,* has drawn authors at Square Tree to her, and she has helped them find their voice while writing their books.

Speaking is a natural progression of the healing that comes through writing a book. Often, an author's goal may not initially be to become a professional speaker, but speaking can be a natural outgrowth of the ministry or business that God is launching them into.

Book's Driving Force

Knowing your "why" is the driving force of your book. God may reveal why you're writing your book at the very beginning, but sometimes the revelation comes through the writing process. Either way, knowing your why is extremely important because it affects the way the book is written and how it's marketed. As you learn the true purpose of your book, it allows you to set proper expectations and prevent disappointment or misunderstandings of what God is doing. The scenarios given in this chapter are broad overviews of ways God can launch you, but God's plan may be far bigger than anything you can imagine, so stay open for Him to launch you in unique and unexpected ways. Trust Him through the process. As He unfolds insights to you, write down your "why" and put it on a bulletin board. Keep it in front of you each day, so on those days where it's hard to write, you'll be encouraged to push through because you know your why.

LAUNCHING YOU

💡 **Pro Tip:**
Ask God why you're writing your book. Remember, some answers may come now, and some may come while you're writing the book.

 **Launching YOU Into Action**
1. Spend some quiet time with God and ask Him IF you're to write the book.
2. Ask God IF you're to publish it. (You may be called to write it, but NOT publish it!)
3. Ask God WHY you're writing this book. He may give you something right away, or the revelations may come as you write.

CHAPTER 2

THE "WHO" BEHIND YOUR MISSION

Sally Ride paved the way for women in space when she applied for the NASA astronaut corps, along with 8,000 other applicants. She was one out of thirty-five people selected and became a mission specialist on the seventh Space Shuttle mission that deployed communication satellites. Ride became not only the youngest astronaut at 32 years old, but also the first American woman in space. Later, she became a physics instructor and wrote books to encourage young girls to pursue the sciences. Sally broke the glass ceiling for other women to become astronauts and go into space. Ride knew WHO her own personal mission was for, which is key when writing your book.

****

"Your Promised Land is a person, not a place," Christian teacher Shawn Bolz shared while I was sitting in church one day.

A person, not a place.

A person, not a destination, I ruminated.

I'd never thought about the Promised Land like this before. Our Promised Land is the readers of our book. They are the WHO we are called to speak to.

The church is called to reach the masses for Christ, and the verse often used for this is when Paul told the Corinthians, "I have become all things to all people…" This is a great Scripture, but when you are writing a book, you must find that perfect fit and niche it down. You'll have to select a specific group of people that your book is for, in other words, your WHO.

"Who's your book for?" I ask authors when I do my Vision Consulting sessions.

"Everyone!" is usually the answer.

When pressed to give a more specific answer, they say, "The lost and the hurting, or people with trauma."

This could literally be everyone in the world!

You'll need to select a target audience and niche down as tight as you can. Niching down is the nemesis of many writers.

But Jesus niched.

He chose only twelve disciples—three with whom He was really close, and one who betrayed him. He came specifically for the Jews, not the Gentiles. Yet, he reached the entire world. Visualize an hourglass shape. The sand narrows toward "the niche" and eventually widens and fills the bottom half. To do this, every author should niche down to at least four different levels.

Amy King came to Square Tree with an idea to help single women fight temptation while waiting for marriage. On the surface, it looked like she already had a niche—Single Ladies. But that wasn't enough.

How old are these single ladies?

Have they ever been married before?

Had they been divorced?

Do they have children?

As we worked with her, her audience or WHO began to form. Hey, Single Ladies became the name of her ministry. As we niched down her audience, she was very specific in terms of defining the women she

THE "WHO" BEHIND YOUR MISSION

wanted in her community.

While selecting your WHO, you'll need to niche down four levels to describe them. Amy niched down four levels in her ministry.

Hey, Single Ladies
- Single
- Christian Women
- Never Been Married
- 30-39 Years Old

Niching down this deep will ensure that when you communicate to your audience through emails, books, or videos on social media, they'll know you're speaking directly to them. They'll feel as if they are the only ones in the room.

Speaking to a divorced woman who's 45 years old and has children is very different from the way you might speak to a 30-year-old who has never been married. Each of these women face different challenges, yet Amy's book will only address the specific need of the niche audience she is going after.

The more you niche down your audience, the greater the opportunity to make a huge impact. As you niche, write down what problems this specific audience faces and then make sure to address this in the book. What are their biggest struggles or pain points? Those will then become the chapters in your book.

Your audience will feel that you understand them deeply when you speak to them specifically to where they are on their life journey.

HINT: Most people attract others who are similar in age and station in life.

As you niche down, you get very specific in the hourglass, then as more people come, you can spread your audience a little broader. Think of your favorite speaker in the church. Many of them started with a

LAUNCHING YOU

small group of people, speaking on a specific topic that they felt most passionate about. Then, as the ministry grew, they broadened out to a wider audience.

As Amy thought about it, she began to describe her ideal single lady, and together we were able to come up with a mission statement for the ministry, which in turn would guide the books she is to write.

Hey, Single Ladies Mission Statement

"I empower single women who feel unfulfilled because their dream of marriage and having kids has not happened yet, and offer supportive prayer groups and resources that shift their mindsets—giving their single season the purpose it deserves!"

Hard to Niche Down

Sometimes it may be difficult to niche down. I used to approach it strictly from a business perspective—until I met a new client one day. During our Vision Consulting sessions, we invited God to speak into her dilemma of narrowing down her audience. She had started focusing on executive women but felt conflicted about leaving behind her "mamas"—stay-at-home moms—who had been a big part of her heart and work.

"Do you feel like your mamas are happy with the services you're providing them?" I asked.

She hesitated. While she believed she was serving them well, she admitted there was a lingering feeling of guilt, as if focusing entirely on career women meant abandoning the stay-at-home moms. We brought both of her audiences to God in prayer, seeking His insight.

That's when it became clear: her struggle with niching down wasn't just a business issue. It was rooted in something deeper. When my client got married, she had longed to be a stay-at-home mom but couldn't, as

THE "WHO" BEHIND YOUR MISSION

she needed to work to support her family. That unfulfilled desire had left a wound, and it was surfacing now as she tried to step fully into her niche.

Through prayer, God brought healing to this unresolved part of her life. As her heart was freed from that burden, she found clarity and confidence to focus on her executive women audience without guilt.

This experience taught me an invaluable lesson: if you're struggling to niche down, it may not simply be a business decision. There might be unresolved emotional or spiritual healing needed before you can fully commit to one niche.

Mission Statement

"Your mission statement will be your plumb line," I coach authors in their Vision Consulting sessions. This will be the foundation in which you base all your decisions for the book. It will be easier to say yes or no to opportunities that come to you if you know where you're headed with your mission statement.

"Don't despise these small beginnings, for the Lord rejoices to see the work begin, to see the plumb line in Zerubbabel's hand."[1]

Zerubbabel was the governor of the Yehud province, and he led the first group of Jews who returned from Babylonian captivity to Judah. He also laid the foundation of the second Temple in Jerusalem. Zerubbabel knew he was called to the Jewish people, and he recognized his assignment—to bring back the Israelites to Judaea and rebuild the Temple.

As you write your book, you'll need to know your WHO and your ASSIGNMENT. Both are critical to creating your mission statement, your plumb line to measure opportunities that come to you.

---

[1] Zechariah 4:10 NLT

LAUNCHING YOU

Covert or Overt

Once you know your WHO, then the question becomes, "Will you be covert or overt in your writing?" If your audience is specifically to Christians, then you can be overt, using Christian terms or language to minister to them. If you want a wider audience—both Christians *and* non-Christians—avoid "Christianese," which will only confuse and alienate your unchurched audience and turn them away.

Once you create your mission statement, niche four levels down and know the specific audience you're reaching. You can then decide how overt you want your writing language to be to that specific audience. Beware of using too much spiritual language, whether your audience is primarily Christian or not. Some spiritual words are thrown around without really defining anything at all. Phrases such as "that's a confirmation or fleece" or "I have a check in my spirit" are types of Christian slang that actually take away, rather than add to your writing. Steer clear of specific references like the *7 Mountain Mandate,* which only certain Christians in different streams of the Church would be familiar with, as well as any denominational preferences, unless that is the objective of your book. It's better to put stories into your own words or choose fresh examples that would better explain your concept.

You Need to Say No

We have helped launch numerous ministries geared toward moms.

"What about the dads?" is a common question we get asked repeatedly.

But the question is usually asked by the women, not the men themselves. For Hurting Moms, Mending Hearts, Cathy chose to focus on ministering to the moms, and the dads get blessed through the moms finding healing.

It's just as important what you say no to as what you say yes to.

THE "WHO" BEHIND YOUR MISSION

After the Vision Consulting session is over, Square Tree editors are given the mission statement to know the direction the author is going in and to make sure the book is staying on target with the author's goal.

Knowing your target audience is also important when you begin to market your book. If you discover WHO your audience is, then you'll know which platforms you can find them on social media and other places they "hang out" online or physically.

- Where does your target audience hang out on social media?
- What types of associations, clubs, or organizations do they belong to?
- What types of events does this audience go to?

When you know the answer to these questions, your marketing is easy!

When we first promoted the Hurting Moms, Mending Hearts ministry, we posted on ALL the different social media platforms, and it became impossible to handle and too much of a strain on their budget. Our target audience was middle-aged moms with children who were addicts. The majority of these moms were on Facebook. That is where our target audience hung out on social media.

As soon as we realized this, we went "all in" on the Facebook platform, hiring a mentor to help us run Facebook ads. After four years, we had *five million* views on the ministry's videos. To date, they have over 100,000 followers on their FB page. If we had been spread out on all the different social media platforms, we wouldn't have seen those kinds of results. We stayed focused on where these women were on social media.

Niche down on four different levels, then focus on where you'll find your niche audience and watch what God will do with your loaves and fish, multiplying them beyond your wildest dreams.

LAUNCHING YOU

Finding the Right People

"I read your Facebook ad that said you have a prophetic intercessory prayer team that prays over the authors, and I instantly knew this group was for me," a Square Tree Writers' Roadmap participant said.

When I wrote the Facebook ad for our "Calling Out the Book" Challenge, I put some verbiage about having a *prophetic* intercessory prayer team at the company. I wasn't sure if I should put in the word prophetic in front of the words "intercessory prayer team." In the end, keeping the word *prophetic* got a lot of positive feedback, revealing that I was speaking directly to the exact community I wanted to work with at my company. The word *prophetic* can be offensive in some church streams, so it was a risk, but it paid off by sending us the right people

The more you step out of the boat and take risks to find your audience, you'll begin to see who you enjoy working with in business, ministry, or writing. Choose your niche audience wisely because you'll be with them for a long time. They need to be the group that makes you get up early in the morning to write to or help—the readers you love serving. Have God confirm this is your group and see if you're at peace working with this particular niche audience. Then pour into them and keep going even if you find a few adverse voices as you move forward.

Negative People in Your Audience

Your target audience won't be perfect. Your readers are human, and each group comes with their own set of challenges. They may say things that sting, but because you love this niche so much, you'll overlook the few who say negative things and pursue the ones who are truly moving forward.

For fiction authors, it may be a fan who simply didn't like one of your books in the series, or that you killed off one of their favorite characters.

THE "WHO" BEHIND YOUR MISSION

For nonfiction, it usually is a group of people you're ministering to who may have experienced heavy trauma and have gotten triggered. For business, it may be a reader who completely disagrees with the advice you've given in your book.

"Hurting people hurt other people" is true today as it has always been.

Are you willing to take the hit from a few so you can still celebrate the wins with the rest of the group?

It takes intentionality to focus on the ones who truly want your help. If you can't take the negative comments from your readers, then it's not the right audience for you. You need to be in love with your audience so much that you're willing to take the good and the bad from them (within boundaries).

"The Bible is the only book I read or need!" a lady wrote on our Facebook ad for the "Calling Out the Book" Challenge.

She was upset that other Christians felt called to write a book outside of the Word of God. She was not someone in our niche audience, so I didn't waste my time trying to argue with her over writing a book. I just let the comment on Facebook slide off my back and serve the people who were our target audience.

It's just as important who you attract as who you repel. In our Christian circles, we're taught to be all things to all men. While that sounds good in theory, you can't literally help every single person. You need to attract the ones God is specifically calling you to. It's hard to see anyone walk away. Jesus had to let the rich young ruler walk away from him as well as many others.

"I want a refund," one lady said during the Book Challenge.

"This group just isn't for me," she emailed.

While we were saddened that she was leaving (likely out of fear and mindset issues), we didn't chase after her or try to convince her to stay.

LAUNCHING YOU

We simply let her walk away and focused on the ones who wanted to be in the group. It's not always easy to do this, especially if you have a heart for people, but it's *absolutely* necessary to focus on the ones who have raised their hand to stay as part of your niche audience.

Find the right niche for you and your books: people whom you truly enjoy spending time with and helping. Stay intentional with them, smooth over the few negative comments from readers who are truly your demographic and see if there's any validity to what they're saying. Let go of the ones who aren't a good fit.

Torn Between Two Cultures

"I want to write my book to reach both the Black and Asian community," Paula Watson-Gardner, a health professional from England, explained to me in our Vision Consulting session.

I asked her why she selected two communities. She said that both communities had been significantly affected during COVID. In our consultation, we discussed niching down her audience even tighter. It's hard enough to fully serve one audience, let alone two. She decided to lean into the Black community, and her business and books exploded!

When you niche, you'll get pushback at times.

"Why are you only working with the Black community?" a random bloke said to her one day.

Again, who you repel is just as important as who you attract. He was not her audience, and he was repelled by her message. That is perfect! You don't want to attract the wrong people, and by leaning in tightly to her preferred audience, she's attracting the right people for her business.

Your Niche on Social Media Platforms

When you know your audience, you'll know where to find them. Your

THE "WHO" BEHIND YOUR MISSION

niche will have a particular social media platform they favor over the rest. As we discussed, Jacke Van Woerkom (Rose) wrote a book and curriculum for grieving moms. Many of those moms were middle-aged women who were primarily on Facebook or attending local grief groups, but weren't getting their needs met. We began running Facebook ads for her groups and had to figure out if we wanted physical groups at churches or online groups. We decided to start with online groups based on everything we had learned from the Hurting Moms ministry. Facebook ads are where we started. It lined up with the goals of the curriculum and ministry.

We also created strategic partnerships, locally. General grieving groups often talk about a parent or older person who has passed away, which is entirely different than having a child die before their time. Because Jacke understood the specific needs of these women, she reached and formed partnerships with some of the other national grief groups, and those women in online grief groups as well. This allowed her message to go out further and faster than if she hadn't niched down.

You Attract You

If you're struggling with niching down your audience, think about things you enjoy and the places you hang out both in town and online. Usually, your niche audience will be someone similar to you, either culturally or experientially. You'll be able to relate to them because you have done similar things. If you're a fiction author, you'll be able to relate to them through common interests. One of our fiction authors, Angela Hughes, loves King Author and anything related to that time in history, so she's attracting people to her who also love Arthurian legend. Angela knows where these people go online, which makes marketing so much easier.

Find your WHO and learn what organizations they belong to, and

LAUNCHING YOU

where they hang out online. When you serve your WHO well, you'll build momentum for your book and many other opportunities that will come to you.

 **Pro Tip:**
Niche down your target audience four different levels deep.

 Launching YOU into Action
1. Write down your niche audience. Make sure it's four levels deep.
2. Research where your audience shows up in online groups and pages, and which organizations they belong to.
3. Ask God if there are any mindset shifts that need to happen around letting people go that aren't part of your niche.

CHAPTER 3
NAVIGATING GENRES

Inspiration4 was the first all-civilian crew launched into low Earth orbit aboard the Falcon 9 rocket. Operated by SpaceX, on behalf of Shift4 Payments CEO Jared Isaacman, their assignment was to train four private citizens to become astronauts. The name of their Dragon Spacecraft is Resilience.

Their multi-pronged mission was to raise money for St. Jude's Cancer Research, and they chose Hayley Arceneaux, a childhood cancer survivor from St. Jude's, who went on to become a physician assistant at the very hospital that saved her life. Their mission proved that civilians could do well in space and perform medical experiments, such as cognitive function, oxygen levels, and monitoring physiological and stress responses that impact the human body during space travel. They partnered with St. Jude's, whose mission is "No child dies in the dawn of life." In partnership with SpaceX, Shift4 Payments, combined with a fundraising campaign, raised over $243 million dollars. The all-civilian crew was successful in their mission, leading to a multitude of partnerships with other medical organizations for their next mission called Polaris Dawn.

****

The mission of Inspiration4, and even the spacecraft's name, Resiliency, were exactly in alignment with the tasks they accomplished

LAUNCHING YOU

in space and the strategic business partnerships they formed. Being in alignment with your assignment and mission is vital so they all work in tandem.

Stay Focused

When the Inspiration4 crew committed to the project, it was a rigorous six-month process to prepare. Your assignment as an author is going to take commitment and a cost that isn't always evident at the beginning. When you fall in love with your WHO, the sacrifices you have made in time, energy, and finances will be well worth it when you publish your book and see it in their hands. God wants to launch YOU, but it's also about the WHO that is on the other side of your YES to God.

Many authors come to us with numerous book ideas in various genres they wish to write. For example, they want to write a children's book, *and* a memoir, *and* a devotional. Since your assignment is tied to your WHO, when you bounce around from genre to genre, with different audiences, you may miss the target God has intended you to hit. All of your books should align with the same audience (unless you are writing a memoir to heal or if the end goal is to launch you into something totally different). Be conscious of a common thread, purpose, and audience; for if you're trying to run in too many lanes (spread yourself too thin), the obstacles (and spiritual warfare) may overwhelm you. Focus on the one assignment God has called you to pursue.

How to Stop *Unnecessary* Spiritual Warfare

"Stop praying over this justice area!" God exclaimed.

I'd started to pray for a major social justice area, but God specifically told me to stop.

It shocked me.

NAVIGATING GENRES

Why would God tell me not to pray over this? Surely this was an area near and dear to His heart.

Immediately, I felt a download into my spirit.

"This isn't the race I've called you to run. And…if you continue down this path, praying here and there for it while not being *assigned* to this area, you'll call down unnecessary spiritual warfare that isn't yours to fight," He explained.

I was beginning to see for the first time that all our assignments come with corresponding warfare that gives us the grit to win the *right* race in which He's called us. As you lean into your calling, you'll attract those He wants you to partner with.

When you skip lanes or try to run in more than one lane, you won't win the race He's called you to, and it will bring unnecessary warfare. The warfare you encounter in your assignment *qualifies you*. And the battles you face outside of your assignment will *wipe you out!*

Too Many Lanes

Spiritual attacks increase as you run in multiple lanes, and you may have enough to deal with as you fully face your assignment. Why bring down more conflict that is unneeded?

"Divide and conquer" is an age-old strategy for success, but why let it be used on you? Juggling multiple audiences with multiple objectives makes you ineffective, crushing what you've worked so hard to build. No matter how great the cause may be, they may not be the battles God has called you to fight.

Remember the verse where Paul says he has fought the good fight and that we should *run the race marked out for us*? God equips you to persevere and overcome the warfare, but be sure you know in which lane He has called you to run. Running the race to win is more than about

LAUNCHING YOU

winning. It's also about equipping you through the process. Often, the specific trials you may face—meant to destroy you—actually become the weapons of your warfare that you'll take into the sphere of influence He's assigned you.

Press into God and ask Him your assignment, and let that drive the rest of your decisions moving forward.

Once you know your assignment, select a genre for your book. Whether you write a memoir, fantasy, teaching, devotional, or curriculum, a clear assignment is vital. The genre then becomes the container for the book-assignment God wants you to write.

Healed Enough

As I have mentioned, writing a memoir can be a healing journey. It may take months or even years. Authors who rush to write their memoirs quickly haven't yet gone through the "work" of healing. We receive numerous memoir manuscripts each year where it's evident the author is still in the hurtful phase of writing and has jumped ahead without the true restoration.

How can you tell if you are "healed enough" to publish your memoir? Well, if you can tell your story to someone verbally and it doesn't have the same sting it once did, or if you're on a stage speaking without crying or having to push down the pain, you have received much of your healing already. However, if the pain is still raw and present, you'll need to work with a Cognitive Release Coach to find the healing for the next phase of your memoir. When you find yourself in that "healing and helping phase," your memoir is ready for submission to a publisher, launching you into a ministry to support others who have experienced similar struggles.

NAVIGATING GENRES

The Mindset Trap

Beware of false mindsets that lurk subliminally behind writing a memoir, such as believing that publishing it will validate the trauma you have been through, or failing to publish it out of fear. Both are mindset issues that need to be addressed. You may be facing different fears as you write your book, such as the fear of being seen or known, or if the perpetrators are still alive, retribution in a possible lawsuit. Or you may feel if you *don't* publish your story, all your suffering was somehow in vain and not redeemed. God has a multitude of ways to redeem your story besides publishing it. A book is only one way. Remember, nothing you've gone through and no work you have done to bring the voice of redemption to others is in vain! If God doesn't use your memoir now, He may later. Your traumatic experiences and all you have written will NEVER be for nothing. God is a redeeming God. But no matter what, writing your memoir is key for healing.

The Shack

Something to consider is writing your memoir as fiction. William Paul Young's book, *The Shack,* was loosely based on real-life situations he experienced. When I interviewed Paul on my *Wilderness Season* podcast, he told me he was sexually molested by tribal people as a missionary kid in New Guinea. He was able to bring the pain of that trauma to his book. It was a way to bring healing into his life through a fictional story. Initially, he made copies of his story and gave it to his children as a legacy piece, but his book grew into a best-selling novel and eventually an award-winning movie.

Memoirs usually encompass many types of trauma, so select what the main focus of the book will be and let the other circumstances act as supporting actors.

What is the main driver of your book?

LAUNCHING YOU

Homeless for Twenty Years

Anthony Brown's life as a child was filled with suffering and upheaval. Domestic violence, drug abuse, and eventually homelessness inflicted decades of damage. As we worked with Anthony, we discovered that he had been homeless for twenty years before becoming a college professor. We helped him shape his story, making homelessness the "driver" and the other traumas he experienced supporting elements in his book. Selecting homelessness was strategic because of its timely cultural relevance in today's news. We knew he'd get considerable media attention as well.

In your memoir, select one area to focus on as the *driver* of your story. Select an area that is culturally relevant—one that people are talking about—to garner more readers for your book.

Nonfiction Biblical Teaching or Devotional

Many Christian authors love to incorporate teaching into their memoirs. A category that spans a wider range for this type of book is the genre, Christian Living. This is also true if your assignment is writing a nonfiction teaching or devotional book. More than likely, God is launching you into a ministry focused on the topics you're speaking about. You can use your teaching to minister to those you're called to support and encourage. One idea is to create video training to go with the book so the readers can do the mini-course individually or in home groups. Another idea is to create a series of books that coordinate and support one another with the same audience.

Multiple Books

Square Tree launched Cathy Taylor by publishing seven books for her ministry, *Hurting Moms*, in only a few years. The first book released was the participant book for the support groups she created. Next came the

NAVIGATING GENRES

leader's guide, daily devotions, and journal. The devotional was modeled after daily encouraging words she sent out to her email subscribers. The women loved these daily encouragements so much that they printed them and put them up on their bulletin boards. Cathy's memoir wasn't written until after launching support groups and corresponding books a couple years later. All her books were also translated into Spanish. Cathy's memoir was published *last*. Ask God which book is to come first in your assignment and the rest will follow.

Fiction Assignment

Many fiction authors infuse themselves into the characters they create. Similar characteristics or personal traits they have, or those based on people they know, find their way into the book. God uses this to bring about healing for the author as well through the writing process.

If you're writing a fictionalized memoir, the assignment is most likely for healing. In contrast, if you're writing a fantasy, historical fiction, or sweet romance book, then God can still bring healing moments into the story for you, but perhaps it's to launch you as a professional author with a book series. These types of fictional works are better suited to a series and industry professionals will take you more seriously if you do so. For marketing purposes and running ads, it's easier to market the first book at a discounted rate, which will produce a higher number of sales for the rest of the series. This is called a read-through rate.

Business Teaching Book

Writing a book about your area of expertise in business is extremely effective in bringing quality leads, increasing your influence, and building your authority. A book is a low-price entry way for people to get to know you and to see if they want to work with you as a client or in business.

LAUNCHING YOU

Knowing your clients' main pain points—i.e., the obstacles they face—can become a chapter in your book. Once someone knows you feel their pain and have the solution, landing them as a client becomes easy. Your potential client feels seen and heard, and the natural progression is for them to hire you to help solve their problem.

Many Square Tree authors have also seen their influence grow by creating their own Facebook shows or YouTube channels to get their message out to those who need it and have built their social media following, some to over 100,000! Dr. Jonathan Clark was featured on a well-known podcast and it built his credibility and authority as both a Western medical doctor and a holistic practitioner.

Writing a business book can open new opportunities in other types of products to go along with your book. For example, if you're a health and fitness coach, you could write a book about health for a particular niche. Then, later add supplements and a coaching program to become an entire brand. The possibilities are endless when writing a book for your business.

Curriculum or Support Groups

Curriculum or support group books are a great way to get your message out to more people and have them interact with the content. Curriculum can be geared toward homeschooling parents, private charter schools, or public schools. This is what one of our authors, Shari Ho, a survivor of human trafficking, did. Since Shari was labor trafficked, her message was an easier fit into a wide range of school curriculum as it had no explicit sexual content. We specifically wrote the young reader's version at the eighth-grade reading level so it would be flexible to reach both middle schoolers and high schoolers. The ten interactive lesson plans were designed based on time so teachers could easily add it to their

NAVIGATING GENRES

school day. Teachers' schedules are so limited with required instruction that making lessons ten to fifteen minutes long and adding a Social Emotional Learning (SEL) component ticked all the boxes for many schools in the United States that require it. As we write the curriculum for the schools in Taiwan, we will tailor it to the needs of that country.

It is important to note that research will be required if you plan your curriculum for use in schools. In the US, each state has its own set of standards that must be met. California, Texas, and Florida, are the most stringent, so if you write for them, you've covered most of the other state standards.

What you create for the public and private schools will also work for most homeschooling programs. If your focus is for private religious schools, you can be overt in your God-messaging. However, for public schools, you will have to be more covert, maintaining an overall redemptive message.

Another way to reach a broader audience is by creating materials for support groups or for individual study. This type of book works well if there's a painful topic you're addressing and solving for someone. Along with the book, you can create an instructional video to go with it, or you can incorporate a study guide. There are two approaches to study guides. One is to put questions at the end of each chapter in the original book, or to create an entirely new book that is solely the study guide. If you put the questions in the back of the book, it makes it easier for the reader to have everything in one location. If you create a separate study guide, then you'll be able to put more details into the book and make it longer. This can create more revenue with the purchase of a second book, but not every reader will want to buy two books.

LAUNCHING YOU

How Is Your Book Culturally Relevant?

For your memoir or nonfiction book, it's best to focus on whatever is trending in the news or in the church at the time. Does your book address some common issues people are talking about right now, or up and coming issues that are gaining traction?

As stated prior, Anthony Brown experienced multiple traumas as a child that resulted in domestic violence, abuse, drugs, addictions, and homelessness. He had a myriad of different issues he faced in his book, but when we met in his Vision Consulting session, I asked, "Which of these issues are the most culturally relevant right now?"

The answer was homelessness. Homelessness was in the news daily and a huge issue in the state where he was living.

For fiction books, what is trending right now in the media or movies? It could be western or fantasy, or space books. Trends are cyclical and often return with a new spin on them. You could put two different genres together like our Square Tree Productions movie, *Infinity System*—a Western Sci-Fi.

Although many of us have "checked out" from following anything in the news lately (and for good reason), it's a good habit to at least know what is trending in society and what people are currently talking about. Ask God if you're to be part of the conversation around that topic.

Knowing Your Book Assignment

You need to be aligned with your assignment, or it can cause unnecessary warfare you don't need, as I mentioned previously. As you find your God-assignment, selecting the right genre for your book is vital in the next step in the process. Just like the Inspiration4 crew knew their assignment was in the medical field, then raised money for St. Jude Children's Research Hospital, partnered with other medical organizations,

NAVIGATING GENRES

and did medical experiments in space, you, too, will need to be very clear in why you are writing the book, and which genre will help launch you.

 **Pro Tip:**
Know which book God wants you to write and focus on. Don't get distracted and run in multiple lanes, otherwise you'll bring on extra warfare that was never yours to fight.

 Launching YOU Into Action
1. Ask God what your assignment is as you write the book.
2. Which genre does He want you to select?
3. Select the driver of your story that is culturally relevant, impacts society, or is pertinent to your business.

CHAPTER 4
WRITING FOR HEALING

The Space Shuttle must accelerate from 0 to 17,000 miles per hour in 8.5 minutes. That is over 4 million pounds that must be launched from pad to orbit above the Earth in the time it takes you to make a cup of coffee.

The astronauts must lie on their backs because the G-forces generated top out at three times the force of gravity, or 3 G. The shuttle astronauts throttle back during liftoff to keep the G-forces below 3 G to minimize stress on the ship. After acceleration has stopped, even at 17,000 miles per hour, you feel weightless.

There's no G-force when there's no acceleration.

****

Spiritual G-Force

The shuttle launches vertically, and a minute later, it reaches Max Q while beginning to turn horizontally. Max Q is the peak dynamic pressure exerted on the rocket (when it reaches the point of its maximum mechanical stress). If the rocket can't endure Max Q, it will disintegrate. To prevent this, the shuttle throttles down its rockets to 60-80% of their speed, reducing velocity and dynamic pressure. Once the shuttle passes through its Max Q moment, it throttles back up.

The spiritual Max Q point and G-forces of the mind are some of

LAUNCHING YOU

the most powerful blockers that authors face. For the first eight years in our publishing business, we saw powerful Christian authors self-destruct their missions when it came time to launch. This manifested in a never-ending re-editing cycle. After completing the professional editing process, authors would go back to re-edit their book, changing things over and over again, mostly out of fear of launching. And for those who made it through to being published, they would jump right into the next book because they feared marketing. And still other authors held tightly to their book, unable to accept any of the editor's comments and recommendations. They feared letting go of control, and it showed up in the final version of their book. Books which could have been more professional and marketable if only the author was willing to let go of control and trust the process. It wasn't until we brought on Dr. Amanda Helman, Square Tree's Cognitive Release Coach, to work with authors, helping them find healing and break off false mindsets, that they were ready to launch and not abort their mission. After breakthrough coaching, they were ready to throttle back up again without fear of disintegrating during launch.

Do you have trouble letting go of control when it comes to your book?

Are you super vigilant about jumping right into the launch, without even so much as addressing one of the many mindset issues you'll face at liftoff? If you don't deal with the G-force holding you back, *God* may abort the mission, so you won't implode and leave a trail of debris behind, injuring yourself, your family, or the mission during the process. When you do the work and find healing, you'll feel weightless, even though you're going 17,000 miles per hour after liftoff!

All Writing Includes Healing

"God called me to write a book," is the most common statement I

WRITING FOR HEALING

hear from authors. Know that writing, especially if it includes aspects of our own personal experiences (including abuse or trauma), will bring about a change of perspective and release healing. Our life experiences shape our belief systems, bringing growth and maturity. Courses you see advertised that say, "write a book in thirty days," don't factor into account the healing part of the writing process. All authors, fiction, or nonfiction, go through some level of healing (if they're surrendered to the process with God at the helm). He uses the tool of writing because it's therapeutic. Healing equips you so you don't self-destruct as you launch into the favor God is releasing into your life.

There's a season of preparation as God prepares to launch you. The longer the preparation, the bigger the mission.

"God, I want to go into the ministry," Kris Vallotton, Senior Associate Leader of Bethel church, conveyed at a conference I attended. God was calling him into business, but he didn't want to go. Kris repeatedly told God he wanted to be in ministry. After wrestling with God, Kris went into business and eventually owned multiple auto parts stores.

"God, I didn't make any money in business," Kris lamented.

"It was in the making of a man, not the making of a business!" God replied.

God was not as interested in Kris's business making money or becoming a Kingdom Entrepreneur as much as He was about building his character as a man. It's interesting to note that decades later, Kris is now in ministry yet using his business acumen to start an accredited college at his church! The business was the training ground for what Kris is doing now in his ministry life, decades later.

This completely translates into authors writing their books.

The book...the book...the book...is what most authors are concerned about. It's *their* baby; they've carried it for years, and for some...decades.

LAUNCHING YOU

It's NOT about launching the book as much as it's about launching YOU!

The book is the conduit God is using to build your character and discover your healing. Paula Mosher Wallace, executive director of Bloom in the Dark Ministries, used this nomenclature in the three stages of book writing. Authors write the book from *hurt* to *heal* to *help*. This is especially true for nonfiction authors, but God brings healing to fiction authors as well.

Hurting Phase

Writing about trauma is one of the best ways to release negative emotions that place stress on an author's body. We get numerous manuscript submissions every year from authors whose pain is very present in their book. They may have acquired some healing with God or a counselor, but the hurt still seeps through every page. It's healing to write while you're in pain, but after you've read through the book a few times, give it to a trusted friend for some honest feedback. Then, allow several beta readers to review it and provide a truthful critique. It's critical you don't take what they say *personally* but be open to honest feedback. Pats on the back from friends and family won't propel your book to the height it needs to go, and neither will it improve your writing. Get professional feedback and continue to improve your book until it's ready for the publishing process. Healing can't be rushed, so let your book keep pace with your own journey; stay in the moment and honor where you're currently at as you write.

Sharing Your Story

Memoirs are the most obvious books God wants to use for healing. In this genre, writing may be at a slower pace as traumatic and painful

WRITING FOR HEALING

memories take time to process. You may fear "ripping the band-aid off" and feeling exposed. This longer timeframe can cause you to avoid writing, and many false mindsets may come to the forefront. Some common misbeliefs are: "I've got to get it just right," "I don't know where to start," or "I'm worried about what people will think."

Many authors shut down due to the flooding of hurtful memories. Increased health issues surface as they pen their painful past; emotional, spiritual, and physical roots are exposed, all part of a core wound. Common physical examples of low-level author pain can be frequent headaches, stomachaches, and digestive issues. Spiritual roots always develop around what we believe, and how we relate to God and others. Writing begins to bring up those unhealthy ones. Many physical symptoms manifest as a "diagnosis," and diseases occur because of this core wound. But the good news is that God is delivering healing through the process in every area—spiritually, physically, and emotionally—to authors who write their memoir. It's a powerful journey that shouldn't be circumvented, so allow the full healing power that God wants to release through the assignment of writing a memoir.

Writing from a Hurt

In the *hurting phase*, as many authors write about the deep wounds others have inflicted, heaviness, grief, heartbreak, and loss may revisit them. Confusion, anxiety, fear, and even terror from trauma may resurface. This cannot transfer to the book and fill the pages of what is being written, for the reader will feel the same heaviness and the story will not accomplish the release of hope intended for them. Overwhelming emotions can trigger the author and others. Allow the time needed during this process.

LAUNCHING YOU

The hurting phase of writing may take some time as you write the book. "Chunking" out short portions at a time can allow you to process your feelings. Don't hold yourself to impossible goals or beat yourself up during the hurting phase by writing for hours or days, which leads to frustration and ultimately shuts down your book's progress.

It's critical that you feel supported during the hurting phase of writing. A mindset or cognitive release coach can help you work through unprocessed emotions, moving you toward the healing phase of writing and accelerating the process. You must learn how to feel safe, loved, and connected so you can confidently move forward toward healing.

Power of Handwriting

Handwriting can be a beautiful tool and extremely effective in releasing healing. Some authors begin by writing their book in their journals. Studies have shown this can be very therapeutic.

If you're becoming blocked in typing your story, pull out a piece of paper and a pen and see if that helps get you unstuck. The act of writing on a piece of paper will tap a different part of your brain and get your flow back.

Healing Phase

"What do you think of my book, *Wilderness Season?*" I asked a trusted friend and beta reader.

"There's way too much pain in the book. You'll need to rewrite parts of it," she said, concerned for my readers.

The manuscript was done; however, I didn't realize I was only part of the way through my healing journey. My first manuscript was written with fourteen years of pent-up pain being in a "Wilderness" season, and I hadn't gone through the entire healing phase yet to help others.

WRITING FOR HEALING

I was blinded to the fact that I still had so much healing to do, until she said that to me. I had to go back through the book and face those places of woundedness once again that I still needed God to heal in my life. When I looked at the book from her vantage point, I could clearly see the hurt poured out on each page.

I leaned into God for healing and rewrote the book over and over until no pain oozed out from me into the book. I still described painful moments within the pages, but the difference came from a place of healing, rather than torment.

"Should I wait to heal before I write my book, then?" many authors ask. No!

Writing is the tool God wants you to use to process your pain with Him. You may only be able to write a few pages before you break down in tears and can't write anymore that day. It's perfectly normal for this to happen as you release pent-up emotions from life experiences that hurt you.

Write!

Get it all out on the page. But make sure that draft isn't what you take to a publisher. Writing through the pain is incredibly important, but this is only your first draft. When the release of those emotions comes, many other drafts are necessary to let go of the hurt and move into the healing phase of the journey.

The *healing phase* of writing is when you've begun to learn to identify, release, and heal the past emotional and spiritual wounds that impact your physical body. You're equipped with tools in your thinking, and as you begin to process your pain, your writing begins to shift. Your stories become more hopeful.

When you write through the healing phase, you still feel emotions. However, the emotional, spiritual, and physical pain has been reduced because you've begun processing and releasing your feelings. This second

LAUNCHING YOU

phase is all about using your written voice and connecting to your audible voice. This means you can both vocalize and express your pain, as well as write about it, without feeling an overwhelming amount of sorrow that prevents you from writing. You're feeling more confident to write, and your writing begins to flow at a surprising rate.

You must work through many of the mindset beliefs holding you back during this stage, such as "not being good enough," "not being lovable or worthy," "not truly feeling like an author," or "can't move forward until you get it right." This phase will see the release of the fears, terrors, and beliefs holding you back and, at a deeper level, help everything flow in your writing.

During this phase, you'll begin to write with fewer breaks due to the overwhelm of emotions, trauma triggers, and your past pain. As the pain begins to reduce, you can shift your focus from your wounds to a more God-focused future, bringing ease and creativity into your writing.

Don't stop after you have written from a place of pain. Keep going. God is using this to bring healing. After you release the pain onto the written page, you'll begin to find healing. Then, start rewriting sections of the book to lighten it up and bring hope. *If there's still no hope, then it's not ready for publishing yet.* We have enough tribulation in this world without reading a hopeless book full of trauma. Every day we're bombarded with despair; we *need* hope and a redemptive message that will attract readers.

God is surprising sometimes. He can use a book to bring you the healing you didn't even know you needed.

Joel's Story

Talking about Joel Fisher, one of our Square Tree fiction authors, and the brother he lost, the sting of death was overwhelming. One day, Joel went through some of his brother's things and found a partially written

WRITING FOR HEALING

story. As Joel read his brother's writings, he got the idea of a fiction fantasy book he could write.

"Write the book. I'm in it." Joel felt God nudge him.

Joel began to write his first fictional fantasy called *Slaves of Swords*. As we poured over the pages together that day, he could feel God's hand beginning to heal his grief, and he felt closer to Him through the writing. God used Joel's book to bring a form of legacy to his brother and honor him. Joel dedicated his book to his brother and found healing through the process.

God can use *any* genre to bring healing, not only to you but also to your readers. Fiction has a way of bypassing the frontal cortex (the reasoning part of our brains), causing readers to lower their guard and receive the hope-filled message authors are bringing to them. Healing is available in any book an author creates.

Helping Phase

"Do you want to help people in the same area you experienced trauma?"

You'll need to be careful of jumping past the hurting and healing phase because it's easy to bypass some of the process and jump right into helping people. We see it in authors, pastors, and entrepreneurs all the time. Helping is good, but it needs to come from a place of true healing. We see it in the numerous manuscripts submitted each year, still in the first two phases of writing. There's too much pain, and much needed healing to fully lean into helping others.

When you come into the *helping phase* of your book, take time to identify, reveal, and heal those areas of loss. When you continue to press into deeper coaching, healing, and ongoing releasing, it leads to gaining your confidence back, to clarity, and alignment deep within yourself. You shift your focus away from pain, hurt, and the worship of your wounds, transitioning instead to worshiping God.

LAUNCHING YOU

Does your book have hope and a redemptive message?

Hope and a redemptive message are the litmus test to know if you are truly in the helping phase of writing your book.

As you begin to heal, you can confidently step out and use your voice to help others. Your focus is now on *their* mission and vision given by God to fulfill His impact on Earth. You become confident in who you are and know your value. You're not swayed by the fear of man but of the fear of God alone. You're sold out for God and have done the deep work that will allow you to write, speak, and arise with firm faith and love.

When you enter the helping phase, you learn you're both an author and a speaker. You become less fearful of being known and hidden. You're proud of your writing and your newfound voice.

When you're in the helping phase, you accept your imperfections and aren't ashamed of your flaws. You're vulnerable and willing to continue to do the deep heart work because you want to go to the next level in your relationship with God, which leads to an increase in your writing, speaking, and presence that will greatly impact the people around you.

The helping phase shifts your focus from limitations regarding money and lack of value to full confidence in who you are and whom you serve, whether it's a community group, state level, or global level. The helping phase allows you to write for an audience of one yet have the mindset of abundance so you can serve many as your sphere of influence grows.

Are You Ready to Publish?

As you begin to heal, you'll want to remove the more descriptive details of the abuse to avoid triggering people who have experienced the same trauma, as it isn't helpful to them at all. When you're in pain, you want to write every little detail of the trauma that happened to you, replaying it in your mind over and over. But when you begin to write from a place

WRITING FOR HEALING

of healing, those details won't matter anymore. Your message of hope is paramount, and it will rise to the surface and become the focal point.

How do you know if your book is still too full of hurt and pain, or if it's now ready to help others? Hope and healing are the focus, and trauma details are left to a minimum.

Hiring a professional beta reader who doesn't know your situation will give you the proper perspective to see if your book has hope and healing. You'll need a trained set of eyes to look at your manuscript. They'll be able to give you professional feedback to ensure you're ready to submit your work to a publisher or embark on the self-publishing process.

Personally, having worked with Dr. Amanda Helman, Square Tree Cognitive Release Coach, I discovered many constraints I had no idea were there. Sometimes you just don't know what you don't know until a professional comes alongside you, lovingly revealing those issues with the help of the Holy Spirit, so you can find the healing you need.

The greatest obstacle for any reader isn't the words on the page, the eloquence of the language, or even the delivery; it's the inner healing journey of the author. The biggest constraint is the author themselves. It's YOU!

Commit to work with God and a coach to relieve your own mindset restrictions. A reader can't be healed, delivered, or ministered to beyond your own personal healing. That is why it's critical you go through these steps to reach the helping phase.

If you publish too early in the journey, the healing available to your reader is diminished. Your story deserves to bring the hope God intended for it to bring. This healing journey isn't for the faint of heart, but it truly is one of the most freeing parts of your journey. You'll never fully "arrive" at all the healing God has for you, but working through the bigger traumas and issues will be the first major step toward publishing.

LAUNCHING YOU

Your readers will thank you, intuitively drawn to the authenticity of your words.

Authors aren't the only ones who need to find healing; companies do as well. For years, our publishing company has seen authors get stuck throughout the process of publishing their books. In the early days, Square Tree would take any book or Christian author that came to us, including difficult clients who never finished their books or who had so much trauma that they lashed out at us at every step along the way. We had to learn our own value as a company and what we were bringing to the table in order to begin helping our authors with their healing.

Two needed shifts have happened at Square Tree Publishing over the past several years. We now have an application process and only accept authors who are truly ready to go through the healing *and* publishing process, as well as books that are hope-filled or have clean entertainment. We also brought on Dr. Amanda Helman, our Cognitive Release Coach, who meets with writers to identify areas that are holding them back. Because of Dr. Amanda, we're now seeing authors smoothly transition through these three phases and get launched.

Remember: Your first draft won't be your best one. Hire a beta reader or join a writers' cohort group to help you improve your writing. See if there is still too much pain in your writing. Have an encouraging yet objective team in place, including a Cognitive Release Coach, to help you know when your book is truly ready for publishing. And when hope rises higher than the pain in your book, and the redemptive message shines through, you are ready for the next step.

WRITING FOR HEALING

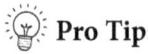 **Pro Tip:**

If your book isn't hope-filled or doesn't have a strong redemptive message, it's not ready to be published. Keep writing until you find the healing to bring hope to your book.

Launching YOU Into Action

1. Ask God if you're still writing your book from a place of pain, or if it's from a place of healing.
2. If you're still healing, ask Him to reveal areas of pain that He wants to heal.
3. Does He want you to see a counselor or coach to help you heal?

CHAPTER 5
SHIFTING MINDSET BLOCKS

Apollo 13, the seventh crewed mission in the Apollo space program, was supposed to be the third flight to land on the Moon. The mission was aborted due to the rupture of the oxygen tank in the service module, which disabled its electrical and life-support systems' coils. The crew was forced to shut down its Command Module's systems and transfer to the Lunar Module, which became a lifeboat for them. The carbon dioxide levels began to climb at alarming rates, and the crew, with the help of Mission Control, duct-taped some parts together to get this under control. In this dire circumstance, James Lovell, the commander, said in an interview, "We needed a positive mindset that it would work out on the Apollo 13." It took mission control at NASA and a proper mindset to bring them back alive. Later they found fault with the preflight testing of the oxygen tank. The activities the team needed to perform before they launched were neglected and faulty. This mission has been called the "Successful Failure."

****

Your mindset is critical to the mission God has called you to as an author. The preparation time *before* you launch is critical to success so you don't neglect crucial mind shifts, which could lead to a faulty launch. If you don't prepare ahead of time by shifting faulty mindsets, then your books, at best, may end up being a *successful failure*.

LAUNCHING YOU

Facing the *Headwind*

As I jumped on the bike and went for a ride at the beach, the wind hit me hard. Tears began running down my face. My mom had recently passed away, and I needed to get out in nature.

Great, I'm facing a really strong headwind, and it had to be today! I thought as I pushed through this fierce wind.

"*You're stronger than you know,*" the Holy Spirit whispered to my heart, giving me the strength to continue the ten-mile ride.

I had to gear down my bike to the lowest level just to keep going. It felt like my pedals were spinning a hundred miles per hour, yet I was only moving inches. After fighting through the wind for over half an hour, I was exhausted, but I still had to face the big hill up to the cliffs.

I pushed through the *head*wind, knowing my ride would be a lot easier on the way back. When I turned around at the halfway mark, the wind, now at my back, I sped twice as fast with little effort. Throwing my bike in high gear, I cruised most of the way back.

This is similar to being an author.

You may face a tremendous amount of headwind as you begin the process of writing your book.

Thoughts like…

"*I can't do this.*"

"*I feel unqualified.*"

"*Who really wants to read my book anyway?*" assail you as you push forward.

Everyone has mindset issues. The key is to figure out which ones you have and to work with the Holy Spirit to reveal and heal them so you don't self-destruct at takeoff. It will take a posture of surrender to the process and even the timing of the liftoff to be in full alignment with what God is about to do in your life.

SHIFTING MINDSET BLOCKS

Authors face two key junctures when these false mindsets rear their ugly heads. One is during the publishing process and the other one is during the marketing phase. Over years of working with authors, there are some misbeliefs that surface on a regular basis for each of these phases in the author's journey. The most common mindset blocks for authors during the publishing phase are perfectionism, imposter syndrome, and feeling unqualified.

Have you ever felt like you must "get it right?"

If you've been in church for any length of time, you've heard a preacher talk about having a *spirit of excellence*, but there's a fine line between excellence and *perfectionism*. With perfectionism comes a host of other misbeliefs, such as the fear of man, rejection, performance, a religious spirit, and pride. One misbelief branches out and creates all sorts of other beliefs that attach to it. When you cut off the stronghold core belief, then many of the other beliefs underneath it will begin to shift. However, each belief should be addressed.

Do you have thoughts like "I'm not loved," "I'm not worthy," or "I don't deserve great things"? Some of these are subconscious and may take working with a counselor or coach to bring to the surface. These start with the linchpin misbelief that "I've got to get it right."

Do you believe that if you don't get it right, you're letting God or your loved ones down? This mindset may have come from childhood trauma or been instilled in you by your family. It may even have occurred during school, friends, or negative experiences (i.e., medical trauma, witness of a trauma/accident). When you messed up in the past, people may have shamed you, and now it has become a stronghold in your life. This belief will show up in a multitude of ways; however, by taking care of the stronghold—the earliest root— healing will begin in other connected areas. (Some deeper trauma may take multiple sessions with a counselor or breakthrough coach to be released).

LAUNCHING YOU

Business Plane

"Your business is a plane and there's a runway before you. Take off at full speed down that runway," God said to me about five years into my business.

"But God, I only have a half-built plane," I moaned.

"Take off, and when you hit the end of the runway, keep going," He instructed.

"That's easy for you to say. I only have a half-built plane."

"That's okay. We'll build the (business) plane in the air as you fly it!"

This has been a true test of white-knuckle faith, because building a plane as it's flying is scary. My own misbelief of having to "get it right" kicked into high gear as the perceived stakes became higher. But I've had to let go of getting it right through working with Dr. Amanda Helman and being okay with me or my team making mistakes. My team was very encouraged when that misbelief was dumped as well. They were free to be creative and make mistakes. I'd often tell our team that it is okay to make a mistake as long as they learn from it. This brought such freedom from performance in the company culture. Most were shocked I'd say such a thing. We began developing new programs at Square Tree because of this newfound freedom, and I sensed in my spirit an entire side of the (business) plane coming together. It's exhilarating and scary all at the same time, but the false belief of getting it right had to be jettisoned.

When you unpack the false mindset that you must get it right, it has at least three sub-beliefs attached to it: fear of failure, fear you won't know how to reach your audience, and fear you'll only have one chance to get this book written the right way.

I've Got to Get It Right

The perfectionist mindset of not wanting to make a mistake will hinder you. This misbelief prevents creativity from flowing, trapping you

SHIFTING MINDSET BLOCKS

in the logical side of your brain. If you carry this belief, then launching into the unknown is scary at best and debilitating at worst. Authors are creatives, which means your brain needs to be free of fear to fully explore and expand in your writing. One of perfectionism's companions is fear of failure. This fear will stop you from trying new writing skills, or even writing at all. It will be a push-pull struggle to get your story out of your head and onto paper. If you're afraid to fail, then everything you write will be tempered by caution and your readers will feel it in what you write.

How does perfectionism show up in your writing?

If you find yourself checking and rechecking your work relentlessly to make sure there are no mistakes. If you stay up late at night worrying about a task you think you could have done better, or worried about what others think about you, these could all be rooted in perfectionist misbelief. This may lead to thoughts like: "Will making a mistake ruin the reputation I've worked so hard to build?" Ask God to show you if you wrestle with this misbelief.

One connected false mindset tied to this core belief is that you only get one chance when writing and publishing your book to "get it right." In this Information Age, nothing could be further from the truth. New editions of books come out all the time as authors revise their work. This type of belief is based on a scarcity mindset. Scarcity is thought of in terms of money, but it's so much more than just finances. You have more than enough time, energy, and creativity to complete your books and redo them years later, if you feel it's necessary.

Another common misbelief is feeling like an imposter. When we ran test ads on Facebook for an upcoming Square Tree Writers' Workshop, the number one ad people resonated with was feeling unqualified to write their book. This is quite natural when learning something new. Remember, everything has a learning curve, so don't disqualify yourself.

LAUNCHING YOU

If you're writing a memoir, no one knows your story like you do. And if you're writing fiction, then simply learning some of the necessary key skill sets is beneficial. Starting out, you will find your voice, and only by writing on a regular basis will you hone the important skills you need to feel confident.

Oldest One in the Room

I'm the oldest one in the room, I thought as I walked into my new mastermind group in Connecticut. *I'm so behind in learning all these online marketing skills.*

So self-conscious, I literally shrank back and clung to the safest lady I could find for the entire weekend, which happened to be the sister of the mastermind leader. Imposter Syndrome loomed its ugly head that weekend as I fought to fend off those feelings, which felt like a losing battle. It wasn't until the third meeting that I finally felt okay and started making friends. Over the years, I've seen countless new people come into that group who felt just like I had—like an imposter.

Imposter Syndrome questions us: "Am I smart enough, good enough, or expert enough to write my book and share my thoughts?" Feelings of being unqualified cause us to shrink back. Doubts rise. "People won't read your book if you're not qualified or know everything about your topic." Any skill set can be learned; you *will* grow with each book you write. This mindset even hinders those with PhDs and master's degrees.

Dr. Evelin Garcia

As psychologist Dr. Evelin Garcia began writing her book, the mindset chatter started. One of the biggest challenges she faced was questioning whether she was smart enough or knowledgeable enough to write her book. Although she held a PhD, Imposter Syndrome didn't

SHIFTING MINDSET BLOCKS

seem to notice! False beliefs are spiritually based and not necessarily related to circumstances. Evelin needed to push past these beliefs as she wrote her first book.

Fear of Being Known (Vulnerability)

"I feel like I'm in my underwear," I remember telling someone when my first book was published.

It was as if all my insides were out on display for any troll to comment on social media or in an Amazon review. My family was also nervous about how much I shared in the book, although it had very little to do with them.

Vulnerability is powerful. It's so easy to say, and yet for many, so hard to practice. We're attracted to Superman not because of his strength, but because he was an orphan, was adopted, and has a weakness when exposed to kryptonite. We relate to and root for him because we know what it feels like to walk in his shoes. It's the same with our stories; we need to "cripple" our character, show their flaws, even if that character is us.

One author wrote about their sordid past, but their vulnerability in the book wasn't there. They kept pointing to how *good* God was without showing us how *bad* they were by their own past mistakes. While in theory this sounds good, skipping over the rough parts of your character's past doesn't lead to the credibility or relatability in your story. How can we rejoice in all the good God has done if we don't know the depths of what He's freed you from? Skipping to only the good "God parts" and glossing over the rough past loses the most powerful part of the story.

When we're writing stories, whether they be a memoir or fiction, we need to be okay with expressing vulnerability before we express the identity we carry in God.

Do you feel vulnerable in your writing?

LAUNCHING YOU

"Okay then! I'll tell every dark and dirty detail," you might say. Striking a balance is important. Make sure to give your audience enough detail to move the message forward but be careful about oversharing. If your reader is exposed to too many trauma details, it could trigger them as they read your book. Tell enough to show vulnerability, but not too many to trigger your reader.

Seen and Heard

"I don't want the spotlight," authors tell me in our initial consultation.

Are you shrinking back because you don't want to be seen or heard and would rather be in the background? If you have experienced trauma, becoming invisible has advantages; it allows you to hide and not be responsible for things that need to be done or accomplished. This worked for you as a coping mechanism while in your abusive situation, but it doesn't serve you well as an author. You'll need to lean into being seen and heard and know that you have the power to influence people for the better, but only if you're willing to come out of the shadows.

Fear of Finances

The poverty mindset is so rampant in the church, it's become like crabs in a bucket—when anyone tries to break out, the others come to pull it down. If you view your circumstances (or giants in your land) bigger than God's provision for your situations, then you'll stay small and limited in your scope of influence. As you begin to break out of the poverty mindset, the opportunities that come to you will grow. Learning to trust the littler things will only help you with the bigger things. It's a completely different level of faith to believe for God to provide for your light bill versus $100,000 for your company's payroll. As God begins to provide, the amount of money will increase, but the deeper your level of faith will need to go.

SHIFTING MINDSET BLOCKS

Have you ever found yourself saying, "I don't have the money"?

Many authors say this to us when it comes time to publish their book. They have said over and over again, "God called me to write this book," but they let their bank account dictate what God wants to do with their calling. The authors who have experienced the greatest breakthroughs are those who gave God their YES first. God then moved Heaven and Earth in wild, unexpected ways to provide the funding for their book to be published.

Financial Miracle Stories

Louann told God she wanted to join our Square Tree Writers' Roadmap, and she gave Him her YES, but wasn't sure how she would come up with the money. The next day, she was cleaning out her closet and found an eyeglass case. She thought it was odd that an eyeglass case was in her closet, but when she opened it, she found $4,000 inside! She had no recollection of ever putting money into the case. It helped pay for the Writer's Roadmap program with plenty left over.

Michelle wanted to join Square Tree Writing Cohort's group, and her friend stepped up to pay half the cost for her. This has now been an ongoing provision for several years!

Andi was an executive assistant working countless hours, but God warned her that her job would come to an end if she didn't start making writing her book a priority rather than working so much. She was renting a place when her lease came due. She felt God impress upon her to go on a seven-month cross-country camping and book writing trip. Sure enough, her job released her, and she was free to go on that cross-country writing adventure. God was incredibly faithful, providing for her needs. Several people gave her hundreds of dollars, letting her know the Lord had directed them to do so. Every place she stopped for the night, He provided temporary jobs to keep her going. And right before she left on this journey, someone from the Square Tree community donated a laptop for her, which was the exact thing she needed to write her book.

Another author had a tenuous relationship with her father, and after she went forward with publishing, he gave her the exact amount of money she needed to publish her book. Marlena's husband supported her in becoming a children's book author, and when they said YES, the financial miracles poured in. Her husband started documenting all the miracles on a yellow legal pad, and there were more than two pages of financial provision written on both sides! These are just a few of the many financial miracle stories where God provided for our authors. But all of them came only **after** they gave God their YES first.

What financial blessings are you trusting God to provide?

I didn't say financial needs, but *blessings*. If God is calling you to become an author, the first thing is to be obedient and do what He's saying, *regardless* of the finances. Each new God-assignment requires you to step out with a new level of faith and trust. Don't miss what He's about to do because you got hung up on the finances or the way He was going to make it happen. The more I learn this money lesson, the more God is teaching me it's not about the dollar bills themselves. Money is an energy, and when you invest it into your calling, it will come back to you in crazy, unexpected ways. Many people are looking for a return on their investment (ROI) immediately when it comes to publishing their book; however, there's a spiritual ROI at work here. Your return may come in a different field than the one you sowed into, or later, unexpectedly. Be obedient to the call God has put on your heart and watch how He'll show up in ways you never thought possible.

SHIFTING MINDSET BLOCKS

Phases of Mindsets in Your First Book

Healing is always paramount in the very first book you write. God brings healing, allowing misbeliefs to rise to the surface so you can acknowledge them and find freedom.

Square Tree fiction author and concierge, Angela Hughes, went through three distinct mindset phases while writing her fiction book, *Elanor and the Song of the Bard*. The first misbelief she had to push through was Imposter Syndrome. She kept posting on social media about her upcoming book, when she hadn't even written one page. Wondering how her friends and family were going to respond to these "outlandish" posts kept her up at night. After she finally pushed through this first false belief, she was questioning the value of what she was writing.

Was it worthwhile or valuable for the reader? She compensated by telling herself that if only her friends and family read her book then it was okay. As she pressed on, her mindset shifted, igniting her passion to continue writing as a career by becoming a professional author. Through each stage of the process, Angela moved deeper into the healing God was doing through this fiction book. When she wrote her second and then third book, new lies appeared, speaking doubts like, "Will I ever be able to write another series now that this one is done?" As we heal from false beliefs, we go onto new levels where different misbeliefs begin to surface, but if we're faithful to continue writing through all the headwind, then we will be a completely different person on the other side of publishing our books.

Marketing Mindsets

"I'll write the book, but I'm going to let God do the marketing." Sounds incredibly spiritual, but it's actually rooted in fear. Fear of what others will say about your book, fear that you don't have anything unique to share with your audience, or fear of being rejected. Marketing mindsets look different than the misbeliefs for publishing. In publishing, it's all about finding your writing *voice*, but with marketing, it's about finding your *public voice*. Whether it's on social media, a live stage, or virtual events, it's all about speaking and using your voice.

Marketing isn't slimy. When you have something of special value, you want to share it with someone because you know it can help them. That's not smarmy. Audiences will know when you're speaking, and it feels transactional. *Transactional* marketing looks like selling a product where each social media post says, "Buy my book, buy my book," and so on. When we treat marketing as *relational*, the messaging becomes, "Buy this book because it will help you learn this new skill set, or profit from others' experiences, or encourage someone to keep going through adversity." *Relational* marketing shows you truly care about your audience, and it comes from a place of serving. People are smart and will intuitively feel if you are being transactional or relational. They'll be drawn toward relational marketing.

Do you have any fears revolving around marketing your book?

Ask God to show you these beliefs and how they impact your writing and your life. Give each misbelief to Him. Then ask God what gift He wants to give you in return. I call this the *Great Exchange*. Then accept it and move forward in freedom from this belief.

SHIFTING MINDSET BLOCKS

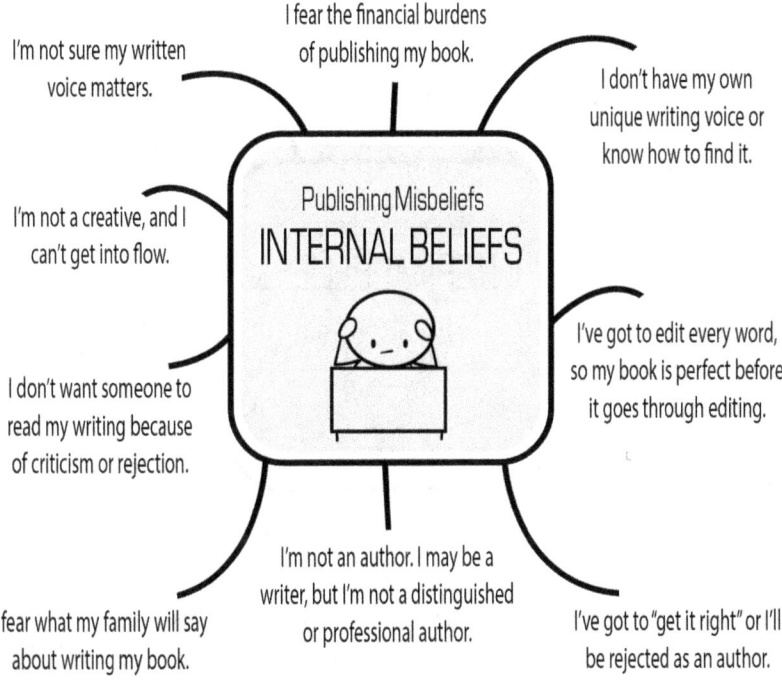

Dr. Amanda Helman, Square Tree Cognitive Release Coach

COMMON AUTHOR MISBELIEFS

Dr. Amanda Helman, Square Tree Cognitive Release Coach

SHIFTING MINDSET BLOCKS

Where Are You Being Launched?

The damaged coils on the Apollo 13 are like your limiting mindsets. If those mindsets aren't properly fixed before you launch, then the best you can expect is a *successful failure*. Your launch will look duct-taped together as you're patching up areas of misbelief that should have been dealt with at the very beginning. It's critical to deal with those limiting beliefs that have become your blind spots holding you back before you launch. As you break free of limiting mindsets, God will begin to release you into your field of favor. The fields are endless possibilities—in the areas of ministry, business, professional authorship, speaker, government, or education. With each field of favor comes the responsibility to steward well the influence, authority, and legacy that comes with that sphere. What area will God launch *you* in?

Houston, we're a GO for launch!
ROGER, GO AT THROTTLE UP.

 **Pro Tip:**

Hire a Cognitive Release Coach, therapist, or counselor as you're writing your book BEFORE you launch!

 **Launching YOU Into Action**

1. Ask God to show you one key misbelief you're facing in your life.
2. Ask Him to show you the root of that unbelief. Where in childhood did that misbelief first appear? Picture Him standing in front of you and hand Him that misbelief. Then ask God what He has in return to give you as a gift.
3. Ask God to show you a misbelief in the way you view finances. Give it to Him and see what He gives you in return.

A GIFT FOR YOU

You've just unlocked your bonuses to help propel not only your book, but everything that needs to come into alignment for your launch.

Grab your insider tips, exclusive workshops, and behind-the-scenes secrets to launch not only your book but YOU!

Get your bonuses now at **www.launchingauthors.com/bonuses.**

LAUNCHING YOU

CHAPTER 6
MISSION "MINISTRY"

Author Jeff White coined the term "Overview Effect" to describe the powerful cognitive shift that awe brings to astronauts who experience Earth for the first time in space. Seeing how small we are in comparison to the universe gives astronauts a deeper sense of awe and wonder and shows how vulnerable and fragile the Earth really is. Seeing the Earth from this perspective gives a new sense of mental clarity and perspective on the conflicts that humanity faces. Earth is viewed with no national boundaries and brings a deep sense of connectedness and a holistic view that all our problems or things we strive for seem so insignificant in comparison.

There are three common feelings astronauts experience in this Overview Effect. The first experience they go through is a realization of the frailty and insignificance of life. Next, they experience a sense that all humanity is interconnected and feel a new sense of responsibility to do something about it. Lastly, the astronauts experience a new-found desire to fight for the future of our planet. Because of this effect, many astronauts have led natural environmental committees, worked in politics, or found other ways to make a difference in the world at large. These effects are long-lasting, and the astronauts never come back the same after viewing the Earth from such high places.

****

LAUNCHING YOU

The Bible says that we are seated in heavenly places with Christ. Because you're seated from this place, you can experience a *Spiritual Overview Effect*, where you come to a sense of awe and wonder and want to create change in the world and help those around you. When limiting mindsets are dealt with, it creates a cognitive shift, and you'll see more from God's perspective. This is when true change can take place. Instead of being about the material goods or your books being sold, it becomes all about what God wants to do *through* you for others. With this perspective, doors of opportunity open that you never planned for, even on your best day! Awe-based experiences are directly connected to peak and flow, transforming you into ways you never expected.

As you begin to launch, there are several areas where you can make a difference. One area is the non-profit arena or ministry.

Hurting Moms Ministry

"There are so many moms who are suffering from their children's self-destructive behaviors," Cathy Taylor expressed at our lunch meeting.

Cathy was one of the pastors of a local church, and she created a curriculum and support groups for moms with child addicts and other self-destructive behaviors. As discussed before, she started with support groups and a participant guidebook, which led to the leader guide, translating those guides into Spanish, a devotional, journal, and then her memoir. In total, seven books were created for her new ministry that was launched. The moms would come because they thought she'd "fix" their young adult children, but in the end, it was all about the mom getting support and setting boundaries. She didn't know the endless possibilities or where her ministry could go but was willing to sit down at lunch to discuss it.

MISSION "MINISTRY"

We decided to revamp her curriculum to make it user friendly for other moms to pick up and become leaders in their own church. As Cathy was already the Southern California state representative for Celebrate Recovery (CR), we both thought it would be super easy to get her curriculum into churches. Little did we know that it would be a two-year slug to get any kind of true momentum into the churches where she had contacts through CR.

After years looking to get into the local churches directly, we decided to go online to see what would happen. At first, we tried to learn about *every* social media platform there was, but then focused on defining her target audience. Once we dialed in that her demographic was middle-aged moms and that they all hung out on Facebook, we went all in with Facebook and started doing some small advertising with video ads. On a small weekly budget for one video that did well, we were able to get five million views on Facebook in four years. The word was getting out, and the online groups were growing not only in the United States but also in Canada, South America, and overseas.

The vehicle we used to make that happen was a weekly Facebook show that she started. Cathy went live every Thursday night at 6:00 P.M. Pacific Time and never missed a week. It grew her audience from a few hundred to over 112,000 followers to date.

Many church pastors are overworked and don't have time to implement a brand-new ministry; however, when we launched the ministry online, we raised up leaders that in turn were attending local churches and volunteered to run the ministry at their church. We shifted the strategy and pivoted to online groups and the ministry took off. Four years later, we had over five million views on her videos and over one hundred leaders.

LAUNCHING YOU

This ministry grew at a steady pace for years. It wasn't an overnight success story, but it was exactly what was needed to withstand the growth happening. We were even able to create a special group for pastors' wives who have difficulty finding safe places to share their family struggles. It became a safe group for them to share with other pastors' wives about the unique challenges they faced as a mom of an addict and a pastor's wife.

A guidebook is a fantastic way to launch into your ministry. We have found online is the best way to launch, then raise up leaders who will return to their local communities and start local chapters.

Cathy said, "After publishing the *Breaking Free* support book, it was the beginning of an amazing ministry that has gone on to not only help brokenhearted moms but has brought many moms to Christ for the first time!" She's now gone on to publish a second support group book called *Yielding Hearts*, about how to hear from God, and the ministry continues to grow.

Cathy's ministry, Hurting Moms, birthed the Grieving Moms ministry, led by Jacke Van Woerkom (Rose), a group for mothers who have lost children (in death) and need help and healing through their grief. We followed the same model as the Hurting Moms ministry with great success. Jacke expanded her ministry to include equine therapy, offering healing sessions with the horses on her ranch, Just Be Ranch. She has now retired from her ranch to focus more of her time on writing her personal story and more curriculum for all women. Her work has touched the lives of thousands of women, both in person and online.

For books and curriculum launching a ministry, starting online isn't only a viable option, but one that will propel you further and faster. It also has the beneficial side effect of helping people who otherwise would never have been reached.

For example, one of the women in a Hurting Moms group would show up online, on her tractor, in a small rural farming town to be with

MISSION "MINISTRY"

the other moms. Because it was such a small rural area, this mom was so remote that her local church never would have had the support she needed. She needed the online deliverability of Cathy's ministry.

If you're launching a curriculum and a support group-style ministry, consider going online first with the specific goal of raising leaders to return to their local church community and start groups. Pastors are more open to starting a new ministry at the local church if they already have an excited church member that wants to lead it and a solid curriculum book to go with it. You don't have to land the large mega churches right away, but as you get into the smaller churches, which make up the majority of the churches around the nation, it will grow.

Amy Sun's Story

"My sister, husband, and I already have a ministry to equip parents on raising their children in the Lord," Amy Sun told me point-blank one day in our meeting.

Amy originally came to us through Square Tree Publishing's "*Calling Out the Book*" Facebook Challenge. She felt God calling her to write a children's book, Heart of the Kingdom. She works with her family in a ministry called Legacy Ministries International, and they had just landed a radio show on *Faith Talk* Radio with Salem Media Group. The ministry asked her to write more books, and she just finished publishing her second book, *Theo's World*.

When God called Amy to write her first book, she was a single mom with $11,000 dollars of debt. She also had a strong desire to give $10,000 to her favorite ministry. She told God her desire to give away that large amount of money, even though there seemed to be no way under her current circumstances. By the time she finished writing her book and was ready to publish, God had provided $80,000 to help her get out of debt,

LAUNCHING YOU

donate to her favorite charity, publish her book, and live off the rest for a season. As Amy continues to write her books, God continues to amaze her with financial provision seemingly out of nowhere, just like the widow in the Bible who took her one jar of oil and filled her containers as the oil kept coming.

Amy and her family ministry have reached countless moms who have used her book as a tool to lead their children into a relationship with Jesus. God has also shown up in unexpected ways. During a MOMCO (formerly MOPS—Mothers of Preschoolers) conference in Chicago, her sister went to grab lunch for them. After returning with food, her sister told her, "Go across the street to the deli. I was telling a woman about your book, and she wants to buy it!"

The woman who ran the deli eagerly accepted the book and then shared that she was an Arab Muslim. She wanted the book for her niece because she liked princesses, but after hearing more about the book, she asked for a second copy, saying, "I want one for my son and my niece so they can both learn about Jesus." Even through all of Amy's planning about the conference and selling boxes of books, she didn't see this coming! Jesus spoke to her heart and told her that book sales would not look the way she was expecting. God could reach the entire Muslim world for Jesus through it if he wanted to.

Amy has since started the publishing process for her new curriculum called *Parenting Unscripted*. It is for parents who want the support and guidance to raise their children in the ways of God, teaching them why they need to give their children a strong foundation of faith, but also practical tips on how to do that.

Your Book Can Go Overseas

"My book just got into the hands of some youth detention center

MISSION "MINISTRY"

administrators in Ecuador and Guatemala," Gus Recinos said, amazed at what was happening with his book. At that time, there were no visitors allowed in the juvenile jail for women in Quito, Ecuador, but the guards were allowing books in. Books can get into places where people sometimes can't. The books arrived in South America through Gus's missionary friends who distributed them to the women's prison. Gus donated the books and was happy to see them being used in such an awesome way. He didn't even mind that some Guatemalans were distributing photocopies of it. He found out through his missionary friends that some of the women were getting saved by reading his book. Gus has a huge calling for evangelism, and his book oozed with that same anointing.

Gus is from Los Angeles and was once a prominent DJ in the Rave movement in the 1990s. He was addicted to Ecstasy and lived a wild life among the underground transient explosion of music in abandoned warehouses in downtown Los Angeles, in the Coachella desert, and on opulent yachts, reaping the consequences that followed. His book, *True Ecstasy*, is about the true joy and peace only Jesus can give, which so many young people are looking for today. Translated into both English and Spanish, his book is filled with powerful stories of how God showed up mightily for Gus and is releasing salvation, deliverance, and healing through its pages. His new ministry, Rave Redeemed, is reaching out to high-level DJs and electronic dance music (EDM) organizers who are forming teams to reach into the rave scene and set young people free from addiction and destruction.

Gus is working toward getting *True Ecstasy* into the rest of Latin America. Gus never imagined that his book would go into his birth country of Guatemala to juvenile detention centers, or that a ministry would be birthed from it when he began writing it. Rave Redeemed is a full-circle moment, going back into the very place he came from and

LAUNCHING YOU

bringing hope and healing to a dark entertainment world. You never know how or where God will use your book or how He will launch a completely new ministry you never saw coming.

Michele's Story

Michele Eich, Square Tree author, came to us with an extensive background as a drug recovery specialist. As we worked together, her niche audience was addicts who have tried other programs and failed. This was a targeted niche that was not very common in that industry. Her book, *How to Kill an Addiction*, has a special section where you hear from real people facing real problems who have overcome a variety of life-controlling issues. We helped her set up a show on Facebook to highlight this part of her book. She interviews guests weekly and has 3,000 followers, and her ministry continues to grow daily.

Michele's book has opened doors for her to host her own show and has brought her before prestigious people who want to open doors for her and the ministry. What started as a book has now launched Michele into the *Voices of Recovery* Facebook show and beyond.

There are many ways to launch a ministry through a book. Starting your own Facebook show is one way. It's an economical way to begin and get the word out about your ministry. For Cathy Taylor and Michele Eich, it was life-changing, completely launching their ministries. Creating online support groups is another. With Cathy, getting into churches was tough, even with Celebrate Recovery connections. Once we pivoted to an online structure, leaders naturally began to surface and started support groups in their local churches. The power of online groups leveraged momentum into the local churches and the ministry grew.

MISSION "MINISTRY"

What Is Your Capacity?

Some areas you'll need to address as you start a ministry are your capacity in time, talent, and energy. If you don't have a lot of time to show up live each week in your ministry, you can record a video series that the participants can watch at their leisure. It can be a companion piece to the book and increase book sales. The options are to sell them as a set or have the reader buy the book and get the video included for free with purchase.

You'll need to evaluate your strengths and then hire other people to take over those skills that are your weaker areas. To launch a successful ministry and to grow it, you'll need leaders. It's imperative that you're good at raising up and training new leaders to duplicate what you can do. If this isn't a strong skill you possess, hire someone who is great at training leaders to help grow the ministry. As your ministry grows, you'll only have a finite amount of energy to pour into different areas of your ministry. It's imperative to know what to say "yes" to and what you're to say "no" to as you move forward in your ministry. Having those skills is likely the difference between success and failure in launching a ministry.

An Unexpected Ministry

With Gus Recinos, his ministry, Rave Redeemed, was born from a book. Books are a fantastic way to launch a new ministry or grow an existing one. Do you already have a ministry to which your book will add value? If you aren't sure, be open for God to surprise you with opportunities you didn't see coming until after you published. Your book will have the power to help people go deeper with God, find healing, or bring breakthroughs in needed areas of the reader's life. Ministries may be birthed, but that's not all; your book may be an extension of a greater mission and launch a business.

LAUNCHING YOU

 **Pro Tip:**

The most important part of starting online support groups is raising up leaders so you can duplicate yourself and grow the ministry.

 Launching YOU Into Action
1. What ministry is God bringing through your book? If you're not sure, ask God if He's birthing a ministry that is coming later.
2. How is the book going to aid you in launching a ministry?
3. What types of ideas or related products do you want to develop to complement your ministry?

CHAPTER 7
ROCKETING YOUR BUSINESS

Richard Branson, founder of Virgin Galactic, had a dream of making it possible for thousands of people to become astronauts. His business acumen and thrill-seeking are legendary. Branson's pledge was to take the 2,500-mile-per-hour ride himself before allowing others to board his new spacecraft, to demonstrate how safe it was to go to space. Although there's now a debate on exactly how far away from Earth constitutes being in space, three businessmen are competing for this new sector of business. Bezos (Blue Origin), Musk (SpaceX), and Branson (Virgin Galactic) are all in a race to put the first civilians in space without NASA training. From Branson's $250,000 ticket to Bezos's $28 million-dollar flight ticket (sold at auction), we have just begun the era of Space Tourism as a business![1]

****

Bezos and Branson both wrote books, but only after they had already launched their companies. Their books were published to enhance what they had already built in business. *A book can both enhance a business or launch it!*

While a book can launch various types of businesses, there are three specific ways a book can benefit your business.

---

[1] Virgin Galactic's Richard Branson still plans to be the first 'space billionaire' to actually travel to space | CNN Business

LAUNCHING YOU

Your book can help you bring in quality leads, increase your influence, and build your authority within the marketplace. People will see you as an expert in your field when you write a book, and it will open unexpected doors of opportunity.

Quality Leads

I belong to an amazing mastermind group called Digital Insiders (DI), led by Julie Chenell.[1] We are a dedicated group who share ideas, learn from each other's experiences, and help each other achieve their goals. One member, Stephanie Dove Blake, co-authored a book called *The Owners: A Titan's Guide to Building a Limitless Agency*. She collaborated with several successful agency owners, drawing on the wisdom of seven- and eight-figure business leaders. Some of these experts had previously authored books, while others had not. They agreed to contribute because of the relationships Stephanie had built with them over the years. The book generated strong leads, causing many to sign up for a sales call with her co-author's mastermind group, which focuses on helping people start new agencies. She agreed to split the commission 50-50. Stephanie acknowledges that she didn't market the book beyond one major industry speaking event, yet it still generated six figures for her business! Generating interest through a tool or tactic can attract potential clients or customers to your business. The quality of the "Lead Gen" is important, and the payoff can be huge!

Your book will help you qualify people who are a good fit for your business. People want to get to know you better before they invest in your product or services. A book is a great entry-level price point for a prospective client to see if they want to work with you. A book pre-qualifies your leads, so when a prospective client comes to you, they

---

[1] https://digitalinsidersmastermind.co/intro?am_id=sherry

ROCKETING YOUR BUSINESS

are in the *warm* lead category. They already know about you and have decided to continue the conversation about what you offer. Most of these types of leads come from reading your book and clients who are ready to buy. Your book has done the pre-sales and heavy lifting for you in an inexpensive way.

What are some successful Lead Gens? Those focused on your target audience and geared for your potential client. But we will discuss this later in detail in *Navigating the Marketing Milky Way*.

Increase Your Influence

Paula Watson-Gardner, a health professional from the U.K., launched her book *Healthy Black Life*. Her goal in writing the book was to form strategic business partnerships and impact local government with her message of health in the Black community. Since publishing, the results have been amazing! Her health coach business is expanding, and she is now running fitness and wellness retreats. Organizations are wanting to partner with her, and she's drawing the right organizations toward her. She's participated in the Black Women of Birmingham Health and Fitness Events, Heart Christian radio in Scotland, the Women Empowerment Health Workshop, and the list is growing. Since she launched, her dreams of strategic alliances are coming to fruition.

What are some ways you want to build your influence? Don't shrink back. Embrace the opportunities that will come. Having influence doesn't mean you have to be a dancing monkey on the latest social media site to be an influencer. It simply means people are open to hearing what you have to say.

What areas do you want to have influence in, or in what areas would you like to change or do good in the world? Write the book being cognizant of those areas. In this way, your book will line up with your goals and you will see the change you've hoped for.

LAUNCHING YOU

Build Your Authority

"I ran blood work on myself to see how intermittent fasting worked and if it made a difference," Dr. Jonathan Clark explained to me in our Vision Consulting session.

As previously mentioned, Dr. Clark is a Western medical doctor, but with additional expertise in holistic medicine. It's an intriguing combination. As we talked further, he disclosed he wanted to start a "collective" of Christian doctors who used both holistic and conventional medicine to help patients all over the United States. Dr. Clark has written two books, *Holy and Wholistic Health*, and a free eBook called *Waiting to Eat*.

He's been featured on several podcasts, including *Exploring the Marketplace* with Shawn Bolz and Bob Hasson. People in the medical community are taking notice of his practice and desire to build this national Christian medical collective. His dreams are starting to be realized.

Building Your Coaching Program

Square Tree author Dr. Amanda Helman wrote her memoir, *Silenced No Longer*, to begin launching her coaching business. Square Tree partnered with her in the "Calling Out the Book" Facebook Challenges, and both the book and the challenges have set her up to be a leader in her field, bringing in many new clients as a result.

A book will give authority to an existing business or a newly created one. A book will elevate your status and authority and draw the right people to you. To solidify that authority, always check facts and statements in what you have written, for there is more at stake here. So, create a firm foundation.

ROCKETING YOUR BUSINESS

Easiest Way to Write a Business Book

Remember when we discussed pain points? List all the major pain points of your clients. The greater the pain point you touch on, the more you'll have the reader's attention. It's like the difference between aspirin and vitamins. If you have a headache, chances are you'll reach for the aspirin very quickly, whereas with vitamins, the response to reach for them is much slower. One reason I believe Hurting Moms did so well with their Facebook videos, using very little ad spend, is because it hit a heavy pain point for moms. Losing a child is devastating, but seeing them addicted to drugs and face death almost daily is heart-shattering. When you list your client's pain points, carefully consider which ones are the most painful for them.

After you have written out their pain points, write their intentions to resolve those issues. Make the intentions practical and not nebulous or lofty. The final step is to show how your product or service will help them with their pain points and intentions, and which is the best solution for their issue.

For example, let's say a client needs to lose thirty pounds. They are *problem aware* because they already know they need to lose that weight. Niche down your audience beyond their need to lose thirty pounds to perhaps an underlying health issue causing it, like diabetes. The *pain point is diabetes* (notice I didn't say to lose thirty pounds). Losing weight is what they need to do to overcome their pain point, and your product becomes their solution.

Write down at least seven of these pain points, intentions, or solutions. Then turn each of these pain points into a chapter of your book! That is the golden nugget in writing a lead-generating book. And don't worry; there are ways to write this subtly without sounding like an infomercial.

LAUNCHING YOU

Book Back Matter

The most important back matter page (the pages at the end of your book) is a Lead Generation page. A Lead Gen here is usually a digital product you can give away for free if a reader gives you their email address. For children's book authors, a fun and easy Lead Gen is offering parents a coloring page for their children. If you are writing a children's book, you can ask your illustrator to create some coloring pages that complement your book.

For business authors, it can be a "five big solutions guide sheet" addressing a pain point that your client has, or a free fifteen-minute consultation. Stephanie Dove Blake's back page matter Lead Gen said, "*Want us to help you build a limitless seven-figure agency?*" After someone signed up, they were led to a sales call to join an agency mastermind group led by her co-author.

Many authors want to entice their readers with a newsletter, but this may not be as appealing in today's market. Fiction authors are the only ones who seem to have true success with newsletters. If you wish to create a newsletter, be sure to add a little bit of book information mixed with some personal author fun facts for retention. (For business Lead Gens, stay away from the typical newsletter, and stick with the examples above).

The key to gaining email addresses is having a juicy enough Led Gen that easily tempts the reader to give you theirs. Once you get their email address, you must nurture that list. This means regularly sending them emails that include useful information or some sort of encouragement in the field of your expertise. Be balanced—send just enough that it's consistent so they look forward to opening it. When they open your emails, your email provider will show the percentage of people that opened them. A good open rate is twenty percent or more. Asking questions in your emails and having your readers respond is great. It lets

ROCKETING YOUR BUSINESS

the email provider know that you are a legitimate company and helps with your email deliverability.

A Publishing Company Is Birthed

"Write the book, write the book, write the book. You have a portal to show up for, and if you don't write the book, you'll miss it," I felt the Lord say to me during my "Wilderness" season. I'd no idea what a portal was, but I surely didn't want to miss it. I wrote ten hours a day for three months and finished the book. I found editors and graphic professionals to put my book together so I could publish it. After I published my book, friends kept coming to me, asking me how to write their books, and I began helping them publish. *Writing the book launched my publishing business.* A business I didn't ask for, and most certainly didn't have on my radar, was a possibility. It has grown over the past decade to not only include publishing authors all over the world, but also to producing movies as Square Tree Productions.

Publishing your book could literally birth a new business you had no intention of building. Stay open to the possibilities as God breathes on your book to open doors of opportunity you never saw coming. There will be times when God will make you privy to where He's taking you with the book, and other times, you won't have a clue. Write the book out of obedience and watch what He's about to do as you launch into new spheres of influence you would've never imagined.

Open Doors in Government

In addition to opening doors in business, a book can open doors in government.

"My mom passed away and she gave me and my sisters such a rich inheritance of wisdom as a United States immigrant, that I want to pass

LAUNCHING YOU

on her legacy and knowledge to others," Dr. Evelin Garcia confided to me at a lunch meeting.

As we discussed, psychologist Dr. Garcia wrote a book called *Mamá Decía* in tribute to her amazing mother, an immigrant from El Salvador. When I first met Evelin, she had begun a ministry in her home country of El Salvador to help people who were struggling financially and had no education. Over the years, her ministry began to grow. As a psychologist, she started speaking on Spanish TV stations, particularly Univision, as a regular guest on their shows. She wrote two more books: *Tia Decia* (Auntie Says) with her five-year-old nephew, and a book on forgiveness called *Doctora Decía*. The premise of the book is how important forgiveness is in our lives.

As a regular featured guest on Univision, doors began to open for Dr. Garcia, first in El Salvador, then in other countries in Central and South America. The United Nations of El Salvador and the U.S. Embassy in El Salvador both asked her to be a speaker at their events. They asked her to speak on the topic of her book—forgiveness. It's incredible that out of all the topics she could speak on as a psychologist, forgiveness was what they wanted. That isn't a topic that is common to speak on in governmental circles, but it's the topic God wanted her to speak about. God supernaturally brought what the United Nations needed at that time, and it was through her book. Evelin also created events and started a ministry called Rise and Shine, with the message that your current circumstances don't determine your future. Doors began to open in El Salvador, with high-level governmental and military leaders meeting with her. Evelin's heart is to bring relief and help those suffering from poverty in her home country, especially children.

Dr. Garcia was faithful in her business and then birthed a ministry to the impoverished in El Salvador. The funds in business are meant to bless others and fund Kingdom exploits. Evelin was able to combine these two areas to powerfully shift the nation of El Salvador and bring food, shelter, and education to help children. As she's being launched, God is continuing to open doors for her not only in her business and ministry but also in a governmental sphere of influence.

What do you have in your hands to give? That's how Evelin started. She took what was in her hand, which was clothing she collected from family and friends, flew to El Salvador, and gave it to struggling young children. Take what you have in your hand as an offering to God. You may birth a ministry, which may lead to starting a business, or your business may start a non-profit. It all starts with taking your first step in obedience to what God called you to do.

For the authors we have worked with, the government doors that opened were not ones they were actively seeking. It just came naturally as they moved forward in what they felt God was telling them to do. These authors were open *if* the government came knocking on their door. We are to be salt and light in this world and bring His Kingdom into all that we do. Apostle Paul was determined to always give God his yes, and that led him all the way to Rome, to the seat of the highest government. And don't forget, Paul also wrote a book, and that book has influenced nations and the world for centuries.

Governmental Influence

"I had been homeless on the streets of Ohio for over twenty years before I became a college professor," Anthony Brown stated in our conversation. I met Anthony at a faculty training at a local college where I was training professors on how to spot signs of human trafficking in their classrooms. His story intrigued me because he had gone through so much as an addict, being homeless and serving time in jail. He found Jesus in prison and was on a mission to create a treatment center in Mansfield, Ohio, called Brown Manor. He purchased an old, dilapidated mansion and has been slowly refurbishing it, getting it ready for his first residents.

Brown Manor was always on his radar, but having governmental influence on the laws regarding homelessness was nowhere on his grid. When Anthony Brown's book, *From Park Bench to Park Avenue*, was published, government officials asked him to speak about legislation for homelessness in California.

This came out of nowhere. He now has the opportunity to affect policies regarding homelessness in his state. Anthony was launched in ways he never would have expected, but as his influence grows, he's remained humble and open to what might come next. Your books may not only bring in business but expand your field of favor in government and education.

Author Turned Lobbyist

Yvette Salinas is a survivor of Lupus SLE and has a heart to help other people with the same medical condition and challenges. After publishing her book, *Faith Leads the Way*, she began to speak at local healthcare community events on the effects of Lupus, bringing hope to patients. Yvette is a Pain Support Group co-facilitator for chronically ill patients with her Internal Medicine physician of twenty-five years, Dr. Donna Frisch. She is also an ambassador, facilitator, and advocate for the Lupus Foundation of America, Southern California Region, promoting national awareness. Yvette never dreamed she would be in the halls of Congress advocating for the rights of Lupus patients.

Yvette Salinas had suffered for many years with this disease, but it was her aunt's final words to her—"Never give up on yourself, and most of all, never give up on God"—that sent her on this quest to help others struggling with Lupus and to pen her story.

ROCKETING YOUR BUSINESS

Once her book was published, she was launched into governmental advocacy in Washington D.C. to help change laws to improve the care of patients and raise medical research funding in the hope of developing a cure for Lupus patients around the world.

Yvette knew she was writing the book to help Lupus patients, but she had no idea that God was going to launch her into governmental advocacy work!

You may not be flown to Washington, D.C., but God may open doors in your local community, city, or state to shift legislation. Whether it's nearby or far reaching, you'll be launched into shifting culture and changing atmospheres around you for the betterment of society and God's Kingdom.

Paving the Way in Education

Square Tree content editor and author Melodie Fox wrote Shari Ho's biography, *My Name Is Also Freedom*, which details her harrowing journey of being trafficked in Taiwan and brought to the United States. After writing the first book, Melodie has created a young readers' version of Shari's story as well as a corresponding curriculum aimed at eighth grade to high school students. We're currently in the process of piloting it in school districts throughout the United States to bring human trafficking awareness to students and to prevent other young people from being trafficked.

Shari Ho's story of freedom from human trafficking has also become part of Christine Cane's human trafficking organization A21's curriculum. This curriculum has already gone out to over 100,000 students! One young girl, after going through the program, realized she was about to be trafficked. The authorities stepped in and saved her just three days before she was going to meet the perpetrator at a local airport! Shari's desire is

LAUNCHING YOU

to transition into full-time advocacy work to help other survivors find the freedom she did. Her books and curriculum are helping to achieve this dream.

Books have the power to create change in this world, in promoting new laws and by changing young lives. Do you want to write for the middle school audience or children's picture books? These types of books will establish your authority in the field of education. Whether a fiction book for young children or a nonfiction, age-appropriate memoir, all of these valid options set you up to be an authority in the schools.

If you write a curriculum to go with your book, always keep in mind your audience. Is your curriculum for home-school parents, private schools, or public schools?

If your audience is home-schooled students, lessons can be longer, more in-depth, and refer to God. If your curriculum is geared for both public and private schools, lessons need to be shorter (ten to fifteen minutes), as they are mandated to cover many subjects throughout the day. If yours is too long, they may not wish to use it. If a Christian school is your target, you can structure your lessons more around Scripture and biblical principles. And finally, both public and private (or charter) schools are kept to time constraints, and you will need to be more covert in your mention of God. Knowing and integrating state standards into your curriculum is a good practice. In the U.S., the state guidelines for California, Texas, and Florida are good benchmarks for meeting most of the guidelines for the rest of the states.

Just like Branson, Bezos, and Musk bringing people access to space, you're bringing Heaven down to Earth through your books and business. Your book has the power to attract new clients, increase your influence, and establish your authority. Your business serves as your ministry, often intertwining with your mission. Through your book, you can reach more people, address their greatest pain points, and serve them effectively.

ROCKETING YOUR BUSINESS

 Pro Tip:

Make sure to put a Lead Gen in your book so you can bring people to you and increase your business.

 Launching YOU Into Action

1. Will you use your book to launch your business, or will your business be enhanced by a book?
2. Sign up with a company that can start collecting your emails. If you're beginning in business, use Aweber.[1] If you're established in business, our recommendation is FG Funnels.[2]
3. Create a Lead Generator (Lead Gen) to include in your book to build your email list.

---

[1] https://www.aweber.com/easy-email.htm?id=503911
[2] FG Funnels Sign Up https://www.fgfunnels.com/join?fpr=sheryl69

CHAPTER 8
THROTTLE UP AS A PROFESSIONAL AUTHOR

Since 1959, NASA's Astronaut Selection Board has reviewed applications and assessed each candidate's qualifications before choosing the astronauts who will go through the rigorous two-year training program, preparing them to launch into the harsh environment of space. Training revolves around three key areas: their health, crew health and safety, and the successful completion of the mission. Even though the professional astronauts will be highly trained in over eight different fields of study, including wilderness survival, they'll still be exposed to the effects of launch and reentry, with the most significant effects being space motion sickness, orthostatic intolerance, and cardiovascular events.[1]

NASA gets thousands of applications each year (2016 saw a record-breaking 18,300 entries), yet only a select few are chosen (only 360 have graduated for space flight since 1959).[2] For the upcoming missions to the Moon and eventually to Mars, they'll need dedicated and qualified astronauts to crew spacecraft bound for multiple deep-space destinations.

****

---

[1] Astronaut training - Wickipedia
[2] Astronaut requirements - NASA

LAUNCHING YOU

A professional author is someone who writes full-time and supports themselves financially through the sale of their books. Your first book is just the beginning, as most career authors average one to two books a year. Like the astronauts, God often prepares you in similar ways; He wants to launch you deeper into the Heavenly realms. Although your first book may begin a healing process, as you progress in writing more books, keeping your same audience and developing a series is better for marketability.

Executive Producer

I met Jonathan Yanez at a writer's meeting in Orange County, California, early in my career. When we met, I was in a stage of my Christian journey where I wanted to hear what God was saying over people as I prayed for them.

"Can I pray for you?" I timidly asked him.

As I prayed, I saw him making movies and going into the gaming industry. I sheepishly told him what I felt from God in prayer. He quietly agreed while contemplating what I said.

That chance encounter was a divine God appointment. Jonathan and I became friends, meeting for coffee several times a year to catch up on our writing and businesses. He is a sci-fi and fantasy fiction author who has now become a professional author.

His career choice has instilled such discipline in him to write that he wakes up at 4 a.m. every day to bring his characters to life. Faithful daily writing has made him a better writer, and with each book, he honed his craft. His ambitious goal of writing a book a month materialized as he lined up all the editors and graphics team to make that happen. He's currently written a hundred books and thirteen series, and he recently accomplished a huge milestone…

THROTTLE UP AS A PROFESSIONAL AUTHOR

1 MILLION Books Sold!

He's spoken at WonderCon, Comic-Con, 20 Books to $50K conferences, and sat on numerous speaker panels.

"Do you want to make a movie with us?" Jonathan asked me a few years ago, after a decade of friendship.

It was this full circle moment when the very thing I prayed for him came back to bless me, too. I felt God's hand on this endeavor and said yes to producing movies with Jonathan and his amazing wife Jynafer.

Nowhere in my wildest dreams did I realize that this "chance" encounter in prayer would lead to me producing movies as an Executive Producer ten years later with him—two sci-fi movies to date, *Infinity System* and one based on his bestselling book, *Forsaken Mercenary*. Because of those two films, a third opportunity to work with another friend on his sci-fi movie has come up, with a fourth opportunity on the horizon. Your Return On Investment (ROI) may not come on your first book or project, and for most authors it doesn't, but it's in the faithful obedience to persevere that those opportunities present themselves later.

Jonathan's launch into becoming a professional author was not an overnight success story; it was over thirteen years in the making. Yet he's always remained faithful to the next book that God is calling him to write. What you do now will have rippling effects in your career several years from now. What you do now will be a qualifier for God opening doors later. What you do now will present opportunities for your family and leave a legacy for decades to come. The skill set you develop and the discipline you set up now will *serve you* when that special door of opportunity opens at the right time.

Recently, Jonathan was presented with an opportunity to write a script for a well-known A-List actor's production company. Because of the years of discipline, faithfully writing each day, he was able to quickly produce a script he submitted to this actor's production company. The director didn't like the first script, so Jonathan said, "No problem. I'll come up with another one I know you'll love." He wrote the new script in a week and sent it to the director. The director loved it! After numerous rewrites, it's going on to the head of production and then to the A-List actor himself, who may end up playing the lead role in the movie.

Generous Mindset

I've seen numerous authors pour everything into their one and only "book baby," dedicating decades to that single project, believing they lack any other creative ideas to pursue. This is a poverty mindset. When we think of a poverty mindset, many of us think it's only about money, but it's so much more than that.

While attending a film festival, I viewed a writer's film that had been transformed into an animated version. The writer had spent over eight years pitching the script, but it was notably lacking in substance and, honestly, quite boring. The audience's lack of response was evident, but despite the shortcomings of his first movie, he persisted in pitching a subpar film, convinced it was the best he could produce. He was deeply attached to his "movie baby," reluctant to let it go and move forward. God has gifted you to be a creative. There's more than just one book, script, movie or project inside of you. Don't hold too tightly, thinking, "This is my one shot." It isn't. You'll need to grow and evolve, and for many authors, the first book is primarily a test of obedience and a path to healing. Each subsequent book or project will improve, compounding with each one you write.

If Jonathan had said, "This is the only script I have," and put all his eggs into one "movie basket," then he wouldn't have had the tremendous opportunities presented to him. He pivoted and had the "generous

THROTTLE UP AS A PROFESSIONAL AUTHOR

mindset" that there are thousands of books and scripts inside of him, and all he had to do was pull from God's creativity warehouse and write the next story.

You'll need grit as a professional author. Being a full-time author isn't for everyone. The discipline to write daily, the tenacity to continue despite lackluster book sales, and the tough skin to handle negative reviews are critical traits for success as a professional author. Being a writer is a calling—an incredibly hard, yet amazingly fulfilling calling. It's one where you can feel God when you write and sense the Spirit moving through your stories.

Fantasy Imagination

Angela Hughes fell in love with the Celtic landscapes and ruins she found on the Emerald Isle of Ireland, as well as in Wales, England, and Scotland, when she lived overseas as a missionary in her early twenties. Her hero in the faith had always been Saint Patrick. He and other Irish saints saved civilization through the signs and wonders of their Christian God—changing the face of the Roman and Saxon worlds. Angela was fascinated by how stories of the saints intermingled with so many of the old fourth-century Arthurian legends.

Angela never really thought of herself as a writer. She and her husband served as senior leaders at a church in Oregon, and she loved storytelling and fantasy, but never quite knew how that was relevant to who she was as a minister.

That is until one day Angela's imagination and the Holy Spirit collided. After a powerful encounter with an angel, Angela's mind was flooded with a fantasy story that wouldn't let her go. She still struggled with how this fantasy story was relevant or important. As she pushed it away, Angela's secret place was invaded. Every time she closed her eyes to spend time

LAUNCHING YOU

with the Lord, she would see a unicorn. Thinking she was losing her mind, she refused to entertain it. But again and again, a unicorn continued to present itself to her. Finally, one day, while scrolling on social media, she saw that a friend had posted about unicorns. Her friend had been taking Medieval Studies at her university and, to her surprise, discovered that in medieval art, the unicorn was often depicted to represent Christ. Which is why the unicorn was often painted with its sides pierced and hooves bleeding in the lap of a maid (representing Mary, the mother of Jesus). The unicorn was a sign of purity and the supernatural.

Angela realized she had been resisting the Holy Spirit! Her own religiousness struggled to embrace the imagery God was speaking to her. If the Holy Spirit had come to her as a lion, she would have instantly embraced it. But because it was a creature of folklore, she struggled.

God spoke to her and said, "I've stories to tell through you, but you must allow me to bust down the wall you have placed between me and your *Fantastical Imagination*. I've made you a lover of all things fantastic for a reason, and it was to write stories to impact the earth with my supernatural."

It was then that Angela knew she was called to write books, and that it wasn't a hobby, but a calling. She published her first book series in the fantasy genre of Arthurian legends and the Celtic peoples. She's completed her third book and is currently writing her fourth.

Angela faithfully writes every day and is consistently posting on her growing social media platforms. She developed a wonderful partnership with fellow author Stephanie Cotta (one of our Square Tree editors) and now co-hosts a podcast called *The Ink Mages*, which is gaining huge traction. The most exciting part is that Angela was a featured author at a huge convention called *Forever Twilight Festival* in Forks, Washington, and she is well on her way to becoming a professional author.

THROTTLE UP AS A PROFESSIONAL AUTHOR

Partnerships

Angela's book led her into partnerships that furthered her platform. For fiction authors, partnerships are catalysts for catapulting you further and faster. This may look like co-authoring with other writers in your genre, creating a box set of books (groups of full-length books sold together), or a subscription model. But as you partner with others in your same genre, you can leverage your email lists, let your readers know about the author you're partnering with, and that author can promote you to their email list. Fiction readers are avid readers, so you're not compromising your sales by promoting another author. And if that author is a bit more successful than you, they'll have a bigger email list to promote you.

Most professional authors weren't overnight successes. Consistent commitment to daily writing will improve your craft with each book you write and provide an incredible platform to reach not only your target audience but the world.

Big Publishing Companies

Are you dreaming about getting signed by one of the big publishers as a professional author?

Make sure you know the facts about working with one of the large publishing houses before you go down that road. The biggest myth is that large publishing houses do all the marketing for you. That simply isn't true anymore. Many of them rely on you to market your own book. Major publishing houses will look at what you already have in place in terms of social media following (some want a following of 10,000), the size of your email list, and how many books you have already sold in the past. You'll, of course, need a literary agent. This can take up to a year to get one, and that is IF you can find one to take you on as a new author.

LAUNCHING YOU

A literary agent will "pitch" you to large publishing houses and try to secure a "deal" for you, but any promotion, travel, book tours, etc., will still come out of your pocket. And if you are given an advance based on predicted book sales and you don't reach your goal, you may be asked to pay your publisher back.

Self-Publishing

I can tell if a book has been self-published. The cover is horrible, the title doesn't make sense or is too religious, and the back hook is severely lacking. Self-publishing is a great option if you're writing your book *only* for healing, and you're not concerned about reaching anyone outside of your friends and family. Then it won't matter if the key book elements are lacking. As we previously discussed, you can write your book and not publish it, and it would still bring that same level of healing. It's tempting to self-publish to save some money, but most of the time, the product is of poor quality and inferior. If you're a self-published author, you'll be on your own without a community or publisher to help you launch. Being in a community is an often-overlooked catalyst in launching you further and faster than you can do alone. We were not made to launch alone.

Hybrid Publishing Companies

A hybrid publishing company will charge for professional services upfront, and many will take a royalty percentage on the back end of the contract. They'll also charge you for author copies and put a mark up on them. In addition, they own the copyrights to your book. Each hybrid company is different, so do your due diligence. Vanity presses are different from hybrid publishing—they'll take your money and give you a subpar product with literally no customer support. Check online reviews BEFORE signing any contract with a publisher. At Square Tree, we have

THROTTLE UP AS A PROFESSIONAL AUTHOR

had numerous authors come to us who were deceived and swindled from a previous publisher (even Christian ones), which turned out to be a vanity press.

Square Tree Publishing

Square Tree Publishing and Productions falls under the category of a hybrid publishing house, but with the added benefit of giving you one hundred percent of your own royalty without charging extra fees for author copies. We care more about launching YOU than launching your book. We have a holistic approach to publishing. That is why we have a Cognitive Release Coach onboard to help you break through limiting beliefs as you write. Authors severely underestimate the part false mindsets play, the spiritual warfare they may encounter, and the need for community when writing a book. Paid prophetic staff intercessors pray over our authors and our company on a regular basis. We have weekly live prayer in our community Facebook group, giving authors direct access to our prayer team. You also always have access to Square Tree for online marketing expertise and our PR department to help promote your book to a global marketplace. You can find out more about Square Tree and apply at www.squaretreepublishing.com.

LAUNCHING YOU

 **Pro Tip:**

Many authors fantasize about garnering a deal with a "Big Five" publishing house, but make sure you know the facts. Go to www.authorcalling.com to get the breakdown of the different types of publishing options, and to find the right option for you.

 Launching YOU Into Action
1. Ask God if He wants you to become a professional author.
2. Figure out your niche audience and your genre.
3. Set a goal of writing so you can produce several books per year to build your series catalog.

CHAPTER 9
SATELLITE SPEAKER

On Christmas Eve, 1968, Apollo 8 circled the Moon. Astronauts James Lovell, John Swigert, and Fred Haise read the first ten verses in Genesis as they watched the Earth rise. Nearly one billion people turned in to hear those words, how God created the Earth. Originally, it was planned that a speech about how there should be "peace on Earth" was to be penned, but with the current war in Vietnam, the wife of speech writer Joseph Laitin suggested reading from the Bible instead. The text was printed on fireproof paper and included in the mission flight plan. As the crew concluded verse ten, "And God saw that it was good," they ended with a blessing. "And from the crew of Apollo 8, we close with good night, good luck, and Merry Christmas—God bless all of you, all of you on the good Earth."[1]

The opportunity was given to them on a world-wide stage, and they seized it, yet the message of God's creation was met with resistance. The founder of the American Atheists sued the U.S. government for alleged violations of the First Amendment; however, the case was struck down and dismissed at every court level, and finally by the Supreme Court. God's voice cannot be silenced..

****

---

[1] Apollo program - Wickipedia

LAUNCHING YOU

"If you are a writer, you are a speaker," Dr. Amanda Helman tells our Square Tree authors repeatedly. If God has called you to write, your voice cannot be silenced. The heights to which He's called you will involve influence, and with this influence comes the responsibility to lead people to God. The astronauts had a platform, a stage in order to accomplish this. What is it that you need to do to "be on that stage?" When the right opportunity comes, will you be ready to speak to the world? In this digital age, there is a stage for everyone, and social media is the first accelerant to boost you toward others, such as podcasts, live streaming, and virtual events, with even greater speeds. The physical stage, television, radio, and movies all give a big voice to the message God has given you. Your book is like a match, igniting it all. Yet regardless of the platform, there are numerous opportunities to represent God well, and to draw people closer to Him.

And as you become known, there will be opposition at times: online trolls, negative comments, all with the one purpose of discouraging you. It's imperative you handle "resistors" with love. This is why setting the groundwork when you're unknown is critical, so you don't morally fall when the spotlight is on you. Be thankful now for the days of obscurity when no one knows your name. Even Joseph was once a "nobody" and dealt with opposition before rising to the top of Egyptian rule—but he did so with integrity. And just like the astronauts when they returned to a firestorm of lawsuits, the warfare, too, may intensify as you begin to take your rightful place on one of the many different stages afforded to you as an author. God has already pre-set your influence into your personal mission flight plan. It's inked on fireproof paper that can never be burned up upon re-entry.

Finding Your Speaking Voice

Trauma has a way of silencing your voice, but as you begin your book,

SATELLITE SPEAKER

you'll find your voice through writing and become more confident. The more you write, the more your voice will appear. However, your writing voice and speaking voice *are* different. The mindset work you undertake during this process will lead you to the next step, which is *finding your speaking voice*. One of the first ways to find your speaking voice is to go live on one of the social media platforms. Because of the proliferation of the internet and social media platforms, it's easy to find a place to go live on social media. You now have instant access to a stage at any time, anywhere, all over the world. Never has there been such a low-priced entry point to speak on the world stage.

The very first time I tried to go live on Facebook, I recorded myself fifteen times to get it "just right" before uploading it into a business group online. I was too afraid to go live and make a "mistake." Authenticity is one of the most endearing traits as a presenter. The more authentic and real you are, the more people will lean into what you're saying because you're relatable. Just like your protagonist or hero needs to be crippled in your story, you, too, should be vulnerable as a speaker. Don't be too polished, or it will come off as sterile and insincere. One of my favorite videos within our community was from children's book author Irene Murphy, who showed up live at her hairdresser's shop with her hair in tin foil. Priceless! She bravely went live, and it received the most comments and views compared to everyone else's "polished" videos. Now Irene has started her own YouTube channel called *Story Time with Oma Murphy*.

Crying on Stage

While transparency and authenticity are critical, a certain level of healing must be experienced before you go on the bigger stages. Authors who cry while telling their stories on stage aren't healed enough to truly help other people. If the pain of the situation is still strong enough to

LAUNCHING YOU

cause a meltdown in public, then working with a counselor, mentor, or coach to bring about more healing is necessary. Your audience must relate to you and not cringe and feel bad for you as you speak. This takes away from that powerful position you need in which to help people. That is why healing is critical before reaching the helping phase of the process. A few tears aren't bad, but if it makes your audience uncomfortable, more healing needs to happen. There are times when leaders are moved by the Holy Spirit and begin to weep, but this creates a much different reaction from the audience. They are being touched, and the audience can feel the Spirit in the room. To be the most effective on stage, and to truly help those in the audience, be sure you are speaking from a healed position.

Speaker Page

One important page you can create and include in the back pages of your book (back matter) is a speaker's page. Your speaker's page must have your contact information, bio, and the topics you are able to speak on. Select a few different topics you feel somewhat qualified to talk about.

I frequently ask authors if they have included a speaker's page in their book, and most say no. When I ask, "Why didn't you put one in?" They sheepishly reply that they aren't really a speaker. After talking with them at length, I find it is *always* a mindset issue, never a speaking issue. False beliefs and mindsets are stopping them from ever considering becoming a speaker.

One Square Tree author, who didn't consider herself a speaker, was asked by a professional organization to be a *keynote speaker* at a prominent event! This was definitely a mindset issue.

Does speaking on stage make you feel sick inside, or are you willing to step in front of the mic, even if you mess up?

Start with a *low-stakes* event. Select a venue or platform with a smaller

SATELLITE SPEAKER

audience, maybe before a small group at your church. That's an excellent starting point to practice your speech. Make a video for an online group or create a private YouTube channel for only those you invite before you go to a bigger stage. Developing your speaking persona involves navigating mistakes, technical challenges, and occasional delivery bumps. Finding your speaker's voice will be a process, so be patient with yourself. Keep going and every event will sharpen your skills. Just as writing and editing were a process, so is the discovery of your speaking voice. Step out in faith, and God will open the doors of opportunity. It takes courage to put yourself out there, but you'll start to break free from the limiting beliefs that have held you back for years, and for some, even decades.

Media Kit

Another great resource you can create is a press kit, also known as a media kit. This includes contact information, headshot photos, bio, back cover info, and links to other stages you've spoken on, including podcasts, virtual stages, or physical stages. It's good to include your speaking topics with descriptions of each, as well as common questions the media can ask about your book and work. When an event organizer is looking for a speaker, having a media kit will distinguish you in a sea of potential speakers. It will show that you're professional. An event coordinator will appreciate how easy it is to find everything in one central location. This media kit should be available on your website for organizers to find you. You can easily add a tab on your website for speaker inquiries along with a questionnaire to answer specifics about the event in which they need a speaker. Questions should include day, time, location, and payment available for the job. It will also be helpful to find out if the organizers will pay for your trip to the event and what the per diem (the amount they allot per day for expenses). Having this information on the website will make you stand out, professionally.

LAUNCHING YOU

Speaker's Coach

Aurora Gregory is a speaker's coach who helps authors find their signature speech. A *signature speech* is a unique presentation that embodies your core message, expertise, and unique perspective on a particular topic. It is carefully crafted to resonate with a targeted audience. Because you only have one main signature speech, you'll get competent through repetition as you make subtle tweaks each time you deliver it. You won't have to reinvent it repeatedly, and the content remains the same. Aurora recommends that in your signature speech, you should only solve one problem or offer one meaningful inspiration or motivation from the stage. Accentuate the problem and bring the audience a viable easy-to-follow solution. The biggest mistake authors make is talking about everything in their book. Keep it simple and focus on the one solution you're bringing to them. If you give away the entire message of your book, you'll overwhelm your audience. By solving one problem, you'll leave them wanting more, which will lead to book sales and working with you in your business or ministry. Have one main signature speech, and no more than three. The aim is to excel at delivering that message, continuously refining it to enhance performance with each engagement.

Power of the Microphone

Whoever holds the microphone is seen as the authority figure, carrying substantial power. Speaking on stage directly correlates with book sales at the back of the room, as it engages everyone present and enhances the author's credibility and authority. A book serves as an effective tool to connect with your audience.

Years ago, we schlepped boxes of books to events as a vendor, and if our author wasn't speaking, we sold very few books. Yet, if the author had the microphone for even five minutes on stage, we sold a lot of

SATELLITE SPEAKER

books at our table in the back of the room. Therein lies the power of the microphone. There's something about holding a microphone and the authority and attention it provides that sends people to the back of the room to buy. If you do a good job speaking on stage, it will attract people to work with you and want to learn more about you through your book.

Aurora said, "The stage is a way to meaningfully engage with an entire audience all at once. You simply can't go into deep conversations with every person at the event, but on stage you can reach everyone in the room."

Once on stage, decide what you wish to accomplish. Do you want to lead them to your book to build authority and trust, or send them to a free giveaway and put them on your email list?

It's important that, once your audience has a book, there's a way to further engage with them, either through a free giveaway (Lead Gen), consultation, or course.

Landing Speaking Engagements

The best way to land speaking engagements is to build relationships with those people who have control of the stages you'd like to be on. Speaking on stages isn't an overnight accomplishment. It takes months, and sometimes years, of forging relationships to get on a stage that has your ideal audience. Each stage is unique to the specific author, their topic, and the audience they're seeking.

A great way to secure a stage is to reach out to podcasters and ask to be a guest on their show. Not only is a podcast a fantastic way to sell your books, but many of the bigger podcasters have their own conferences, which can lead to speaking live at their event. Guesting on a podcast helps you get to know the podcaster better and begin to build a relationship. People value their stages and only let others speak that they know they can trust. Ensure you provide substantial value during the podcast, and after the show, ask if they can recommend you to others for their podcasts. Once you land one podcast, you can keep the momentum going by asking that one simple question at the end of each show. The adage that you are the sum of the five people you hang around with the most is very true. One podcaster may introduce you to others in their circle. Many will be at the same level you are in terms of downloads and followers. However, I have had success with "leveling up" in podcasts, as people have introduced me to other podcasters who were more well-known than themselves. There are a few "levers" in marketing your book that really move the needle in terms of book sales, and podcasts are at the top of that list. Podcasts not only help book sales, but leverage speaking opportunities as well, making this a winning strategy.

Common Mistakes

One common mistake that speakers fall into is the comparison game. Once you have landed a stage, be careful not to compare yourself to other speakers. This isn't fair to you or the person you're comparing yourself to, as that speaker may have been on stages for years or even decades. At some point in time, they were exactly where you are now. Be patient and kind to yourself and be okay with starting out and learning through the process.

Sharing too many personal stories is another common mistake. This also makes the audience uncomfortable. Share enough to show vulnerability, but not too much that people squirm in their seats from discomfort. Aurora's tip is to share what you would tell a stranger meeting them for the first time in the line at a grocery store. This will be a good gauge to know if you're oversharing.

SATELLITE SPEAKER

Final Speaker Tip

Take your signature speech and break it into smaller parts so you can speak at different types of events with different lengths of allotted time. Create a forty-five-minute, thirty-minute, fifteen-minute, ten-minute, and five-minute version based on your signature speech. There are so many more amazing speaker tips from Aurora, and you can listen to the rest of them on the *Launching Authors' Podcast*.

In her closing words in our interview, Aurora said, "Give yourself permission to dream. Be open to where your book will take you. Dream bigger because there's more opportunity than you realize."

Launch Warning

The worst book you can write is one that is a runaway hit, but you don't have the foundation, spiritual healing, or capacity to handle the growth that is about to strike, so you implode. The biggest roadblock that will cap your launch is the constraints of you as a leader.

As a writer, you're a leader. It's critical to the mission to make sure you have a mentor or coach along the way to break off any type of blind spot hindrances. Many leaders feel they've arrived or are too busy to work on their own mindsets that are blocking them from that next level. Always be open to learning and to the healing God has available to you. If you're a stagnant leader, you will create a dormant pool, limiting your community to your own breakthroughs or revelations. Your aim is to be a dynamic leader and speaker who creates a river that will flow in both your writing and leadership, and your communities will continue to rise together to new heights.

Commit to being humble and a life-long God-learner and invest in a seasoned mentor. In doing so, new heights will open in business, ministry, or as a professional author to accomplish the mission that God has for you.

LAUNCHING YOU

 **Pro Tip:**
Hire a Cognitive Release Coach to help you break off any limiting beliefs which revolve around speaking, and any other limiting mindsets that will keep you stuck when you launch your book.

🚀 **Launching YOU Into Action**
1. Your writing voice and speaking voice are both unique and distinct. Have you found your writing voice? Have you crafted your speaking voice?
2. Ask God to help you with different ways to find your audible voice.
3. Prayerfully consider where God wants you to begin speaking first. It may be in your local community, business events, or podcasts. Also, going live on social media platforms is a great way to start.

A GIFT FOR YOU

You've just unlocked your bonuses to help propel not only your book, but everything that needs to come into alignment for your launch.

Grab your insider tips, exclusive workshops, and behind-the-scenes secrets to launch not only your book but YOU!

Get your bonuses now at **www.launchingauthors.com/bonuses.**

LAUNCHING BEYOND

CHAPTER 10
NAVIGATING THE MARKETING MILKY WAY

NASA's Voyager 1 spacecraft has gone the furthest in space in our lifetime. It was launched in 1977 to fly by Jupiter and Saturn, and in August 2012, it entered interstellar space and continues to collect data for scientists to study these planets. Over 100,000 light-years away are billions of stars[1] that stretch across the night sky and make up the Milky Way. "No human-made object has ever left the Milky Way. The distances involved are enormous, stretching the limits of current technology and understanding." Countless stars make up this band of light, but they are too faint to be individually distinguished by the naked eye. Each star is important and beautifully woven together to traverse the sky.[2]

****

In marketing, like the countless stars, there are endless touch points to reach people with your books, products, or ministry. As I was having dinner with my mentor, Julie Chenell, CEO of FG Funnels, and a small group of business owners, she explained the ways people came to join her

---

[1] Has Anything Ever Left teh Milky Way? | New Space Economy
[2] Voyager 1 - NASA Science Has anything ever left the Milky Way galaxy? | New Space Economy

LAUNCHING YOU

Digital Insiders Mastermind group. As she continued, I shook my head "no" to all of them. Finally, she asked, "How did *you* find me?"

"The screensaver on your computer," I said, matter-of-factly.

When I first encountered Julie Chenell, it was at a conference where I ended up buying one of her courses. As she was teaching, a computer in the background of her video had a screensaver that said Digital Insiders (DI) across the length of the monitor. I researched DI to find out more information and applied to them that very same week![1] The lesson of the story? Even the smallest marketing touch points can have powerful effects! Although I found Julie through a screensaver, there are more predictable ways to market your books, services, or ministry.

Sadly, some authors won't do *anything*!

"I'll write the book, and God will be my marketer," I've heard too many authors say.

While this initially sounds spiritual, if you think about that statement, it doesn't make sense. God didn't write the book, so why put it on Him to market it? This kind of thinking is a false mindset, which needs shifting as you move from publishing to marketing. Not wanting to do marketing is a *mindset* issue, not a *marketing* issue. That's why it's critical to work on both the writing skills and mindset issues together at the very beginning of the process.

We have discussed many common mindset issues in the publishing process, such as: imposter syndrome, feeling unqualified, or fear of being seen. However, when these mindsets are broken off during publishing, a whole new set of marketing misbeliefs begins to emerge and need to be broken off as well, such as poverty mindset, false belief that marketing is slimy, or fear of being unable to learn the skills of marketing.

---

[1] https://digitalinsidersmastermind.co/intro?am_id=sherry

NAVIGATING THE MARKETING MILKY WAY

When my book, *Wilderness Season*, was published, I thought, "I just want to give away my book for free to anyone I can."

Since being in a "Wilderness" season is such a "dark night of the soul" experience, I wanted to help as many people as I could. While initially this sounds spiritual, it was rooted in undervaluing myself. Through Dr. Amanda's coaching, I've begun to work on knowing my value and what I bring to the table with both my readers and my clients.

One day in church while talking to a lady who was in her "Wilderness" season, I reached to give her my book. That's when the Lord stopped me and sternly said, "Don't give her a free copy of your book; she needs to pay for it to see the value in it."

Each of us have paid a price for the gifts, talents, and anointings that God has given us. There was a fourteen-year price tag associated with my time in the "Wilderness," including the revelations I received during that time, which have incredible value and worth.

Many authors, especially women, give away their time, books, and products without charging and then put a spiritual label on it. When you begin to know your value, then offering it to someone else for a charge is both necessary and honorable. I've been given many books for free that I didn't read or value, simply because I didn't pay for them. Sure, there will be times when the Holy Spirit prompts us to give something away, but if you're constantly afraid of charging people, then it's a mindset issue, not a marketing issue, and it's rooted in not knowing your value.

Hire a Marketing Company

"I just want to offload all my marketing to this other company," a prospective client said to me on a consulting call.

He proceeded to give me the name of the company and the package they were offering him. As our team dived into all the items line-by-line included in this package, it was obvious they were not truly giving him the value he was perceiving. One of the areas they were going to manage for him was his social media presence on several different platforms. While this sounds good in theory, if an author has not found their own voice through social media, then it's not possible for another person, let alone a company, to mimic that voice.

Take the time to find your written voice for social media, branding colors, and your media strategy, and let it grow, before offloading it later. If you don't find your voice in writing and on social media first, it will convey the wrong messaging, sound disjointed, or come across as AI (Artificial Intelligence). None of these make the reader feel seen, heard, or understood. It's through experimentation and writing that you'll find your social media voice.

Readers can sense when posted content is authentic, real, and transparent. Transparency will draw in your reader even more than having things perfectly laid out every time. One of our authors, Katie Mathews, is a quadriplegic. She posted an unboxing video in our Facebook community. Unboxing is a video of an author opening their book for the very first time. Not fearing to be vulnerable and authentic, Katie struggled to open the Amazon package because of her disability. Her excitement and gratefulness were sincere. It was endearing to her audience and her message. One of the most powerful shifts you can make is to move from thinking it's all about you to focusing on serving your reader.

If a reader senses that you're pouring into them and you truly care, this will be a complete game-changer in terms of sales and ease of marketing.

Seen – Heard – Understood

The *Know, Like, and Trust* factor (people won't buy from you unless

NAVIGATING THE MARKETING MILKY WAY

they know, like, and trust you) has been the bedrock of all marketing courses, not just for years but for decades! The crux is that your reader or clients need to feel they know you, like you, and trust you before they buy from you. However, the saying has now shifted! *Seen, Heard, and Understood* is the new motto. It's no longer about the author, speaker, or guru—*it's about the reader* who's consuming your content. The focus has shifted. The reader needs to feel seen, heard, and understood. That stance carries humility and servanthood, which can take the fear out of marketing. Truly serving the reader doesn't feel slimy, but helpful.

As you write your books, know that the focus has shifted in this season. If you're writing a memoir, it's not all about you! That may seem counterintuitive, and you might say, "Of course it's all about me; it's a memoir." But there are ways to write a memoir that make you relatable to your audience so that THEY feel seen, heard, and known. Cathy Taylor's memoir was published after she had started her support groups, so her community was already endeared to her. Yet the way she wrote it made other hurting moms feel like she understood what they were going through.

In marketing, your target demographic wants to know that you care. Most of the time, an author's target audience is similar to their own demographic and interests. This makes it easy to know their pain points, wants, and desires.

Social media can be a starting point to allow your readers to feel seen. Your posts shouldn't always revolve around you, but rather about the pain points or desires of your readers. When you press into the core areas that matter the most to them, they'll feel seen. So, comment regularly on the posts of your readers to let them feel heard.

As with Cathy Taylor's Hurting Moms ministry, she created a Facebook show and went live each week faithfully for over seven years. She interviewed other moms who were experiencing the same hurt over their children. Cathy was giving back to her community, and they responded in droves.

Your social media posts shouldn't look like "buy my book...buy my book...buy my book" for every single post; instead, they should revolve around giving value.

There's an amazing book called *Jab, Jab, Right Hook* by Gary Vaynerchuk. Jabs are the value you provide as a company to your customers for free, or, in the case of a nonfiction author, the extra value you provide to your readers in the form of social media content, guidebooks, or checklists. It's your *give*. It can be maps or extra stories if you're a fiction author. It's extra content you are giving to your audience to convey your appreciation, knowledge, or goodwill. Conversely, the right hook is the ask. This is when you ask a reader for their email, sale of a book or product, or for a donation. You need to have mostly *gives* (jabs) before you *ask* (right hook). If you're a nonfiction author, posts encouraging your readers through the problems they're facing go far in helping them feel seen and understood. If you're a fiction author, posts of fun world-building adventures are what that audience is looking for. Behind-the-scenes type posts are great for both types of authors. No matter which approach you take, it needs to come from a pure heart to give. People can see right through insincerity and will feel used.

Lead Generation (Lead Gens)

Lead Gens, as previously discussed, are a great way to begin and develop a relationship with your readers and is one of the best ways to bring in leads to your business and curate an email list. Remember, a Lead Gen is something you can give away to your audience in exchange for their email address. Amazon is the biggest retailer of books and is king in their category. For Amazon, the value isn't in selling the books as

NAVIGATING THE MARKETING MILKY WAY

much as it's about collecting all the buyer's data. Amazon gets the reader's name, contact, and credit card information and doesn't share it with you. Amazon knows the value of a client is in having all their information. Your goal is to get readers to give you their information so you can follow up with them.

The first step: decide which type of Lead Gen you'd like to create. If you're a nonfiction author, tip sheets, checklists, or helpful guidebooks are great ideas. If you're a fiction author, a second complementary short story that adds more value to the first story is a good idea. As we know, creating something that can be given to the reader virtually as an attachment in an email is the best and easiest. Take time to make sure the document being created is valuable enough to a reader that they give you their email address. A "fluff" piece won't give a good first impression. If you give your reader great value right from the start for free, you'll set a good precedent for them to work with you or buy from you in the future.

"If this person or company can send me this type of value for free, just think of what they'll send me when I pay them." It's the sentiment the readers will feel when you've taken the time to develop something special.

One Square Tree Lead Gen is the *Publishing Process Guidebook*. It took the Square Tree team ten hours to collaborate and gather all the information in that guidebook. Because it has immense value, prospective clients perceive that all of our other products carry that same quality.

You will need a company to host all the email addresses you collect so your Lead Gen is fully functional. We recommend Aweber[2] and offer an easy-to-use workshop to get you started. Once you create your Lead Gen, it's time to test it and see how well it does in terms of people signing up. Create a few different Lead Gens and test them to see which ones do the best.

---

[2] https://www.aweber.com/easy-email.htm?id=503911

LAUNCHING YOU

Nurture Your Email List

As I briefly mentioned in chapter 7, "nurturing" your email list by regularly reaching out to your readers is vital. Consistent communication with your audience will help make them feel understood. Encouraging them or offering valuable information and making sure you reply if someone takes the time to respond to your initial email builds trust. Forgetting to communicate or nurture your email list is one of the biggest mistakes a new author can make. Think of your readers as those who truly need what you have to offer. When communicating with them in this way, it won't feel so scary or insincere to market to your readers. When you offer what will help others and transform lives, marketing isn't seen as spammy and slimy, but simply sharing with your readers something they would enjoy and benefit from, and emailing is a great way to do this.

Back Matter

The easiest way to market inside a book is in the back matter. Here you can put advertisements, resources, and ways to reach them. As discussed, creating a Lead Gen to capture readers' emails is essential here. Additionally, you can strategically put your Lead Gens throughout the book, ensuring they are enticing and appropriate. For example, in his book, *Story Brand,* Donald Miller provides various templates (Lead Gens) tailored for specific chapter topics.

Products Page

The back matter can also include a products page. This page shows what products you have available for your reader to buy. If you have a sales funnel, offer them the first product in your funnel and then the reader can ascend into the other higher-level products or read the other books in your series.

NAVIGATING THE MARKETING MILKY WAY

Amazon Review Page

Amazon reviews are critical for book sales. In the back matter, ask readers to write a review on Amazon. According to Amazon's rules, you may not give an incentive of any kind in requesting a review; however, the rules change all the time, so check on Amazon's site for the most current ones. Although you can't ask your readers to write an *excellent* review, you can encourage them to leave an *honest* review. Compose this request as heartfelt and sincere as you can.

Speaker's Page

You will remember we discussed at length the speaker's page in chapter 9. Key elements on this page are a headshot photo of you, the topics you can speak about, and contact information. A well-crafted speaker's page, especially with strong hooks for the title of their speeches, is essential to booking events as a speaker.

Also By Author Page

Coming Soon or *Also By Author* pages are important additions if you have more than one book available for purchase or one that is in the publishing process. Be sure to include a picture of each book as well as a link to where the reader can buy them.

Bio

On the back cover jacket of most books is a short bio of the author. Creating an interesting bio is another way to connect with your reader. I feel many author bios are extremely boring and fact-driven or filled with the same trite wording, stating their name, how they're a loving parent, have a dog, and live in a certain part of the country. Of course, there is nothing wrong with sharing this information, but spice it up a bit to

LAUNCHING YOU

make it sound interesting and like someone people would want to meet. Humor is a great way to bring interest to a bio. If the book is for business, then it may need to be a little more formal and showcase the degrees and awards, but still make it personable and intriguing.

Melodie Fox's bio is a great example of bringing in professionalism, but in her last sentence, she brings levity and humor, making her sound like someone who would be fun to know or work with.

"*Melodie Fox, editor and writing coach for Square Tree Publishing, divides her time between editing, coaching, and teaching science for a local non-profit educational foundation. Author of My Name Is Also Freedom, Melodie loves combining her creative talents with teaching tools, equipping writers, and inspiring people. Musician and cat aficionado, Melodie adds 'squirrel whisperer' to her list of accomplishments.*"

On Amazon, Jonathan's author page features both a professional and fun bio, while also offering ways for readers to connect with his community. He directs them to his website and community hub, which are key to engaging his readers. Here is Jonathan's Amazon author page.

International bestselling author, check.
USA Today bestselling author, check.
Writing wild tales since 2012, check, check.
I'm Jonathan, a husband, father, and writer. I write because that's what I was born to do, and I love doing it. Because of the support from awesome people like you, I get to do it full-time.
Connecting with fellow lovers of the written word is important to me so please join the Pack via my website at www.jonathan-yanez.com where you can grab an exclusive story or hang out with us at www.facebook.com/groups/jonathansreadingwolves
Hope you decide to stay in touch,
Jonathan

NAVIGATING THE MARKETING MILKY WAY

At the bottom of the bio, make sure to put your contact information to reach you, your company, or your community. Select a URL or domain name that won't change years from now. It's better to change the website later than to go back and change links in a book, because older editions will always be floating around in circulation. You always want a way for readers to be able to reach you.

Back Cover

On the back of your book cover will be a brief description of what your book is about. It should begin with a great hook. Something to draw the reader immediately into the action of the story. Dialogue in the first sentence is one great way to do this. If it's a teaching book, start with a short story to pique the reader's interest. Ensure your book's back cover description is powerful; most editors can assist you with this.

Table of Contents

When buying a book, a reader will first look at the cover to see if it draws them in. Then they'll turn over the book and read the back cover. If you have been successful up to this point, the next thing the reader will do is look at the table of contents. For non-fiction books, each of your chapter titles should be intriguing and stand alone, enough to draw in the reader. Each chapter title can be a separate topic you can also speak about. Media bookers may look at your book and your chapter titles for ideas on what you can speak about on their show or podcasts. Remember to incorporate your signature speech that we previously discussed and ensure that its title is included in your table of contents.

LAUNCHING YOU

 Pro Tip:

Create a high-value lead generation tool that takes significant effort to develop and include it in your book. As an added bonus, consider creating multiple Lead Gens that naturally align with different chapters of your book.

 Launch YOU Into Action

1. Create at least two Lead Gens and make sure you can deliver them via email. Put them in the front and back of the book. Make sure to look at the data to see which one is working the best.
2. Set up your email list and write your first five "nurture" emails. Set an interval at which to send them, such as once a week, twice a month, or once a month. The more often you stay in touch with your readers, the better.
3. Seek God's guidance on whether you're giving away too much for free and consider how it relates to your perception of your own value.

CHAPTER 11
COMMUNITY LAUNCHPAD

The Magellan spacecraft, developed by NASA, was designed to return detailed radar imagery and maps of Venus's terrain. Known as Earth's "sister planet," Venus intrigued scientists who were eager to compare it with our own planet. The Space Shuttle Atlantis launched Magellan into space, igniting its solid-fuel motor for a 15-month journey to Venus. Upon arrival, Magellan spent four years orbiting the planet, providing detailed reports on its terrain and atmosphere back to NASA.

Just as the Space Shuttle Atlantis, named after a historic seafaring vessel that mapped the ocean floor, launched Magellan, one spacecraft's mission can propel another with a similar goal. Magellan's mission to map Venus was made possible by the momentum and support of its predecessor, demonstrating how one spacecraft can catapult another toward its mission and objectives.[1]

****

Writing may be a solo activity, but it takes a team effort and an entire community to fully launch you. That is why authors who self-publish by themselves don't do so well. You need a community with similar goals. A true writing community will propel each author so they build upon the successes of the one that came before.

---

[1] Magellan - NASA Science

LAUNCHING YOU

Square Tree Writing Coach Melodie Fox once had a vision during prayer of a staircase. Each step held a different author's book, stacked upon the other, reaching high into the sky. If you're writing, launching, and marketing alone, then the heights to which you can attain are limited. But in a community of like-minded Kingdom authors, the sky's the limit. Each author and mentor can give valuable feedback throughout the entire journey of publishing, launching, and marketing a book.

What Writing Community Are You In?

It's crucial to be part of a community where support extends beyond words of encouragement. Ideally, this community should include individuals who take risks, challenge false mindsets, and are willing to lend a helping hand to others around them. In our Square Tree writers' cohorts, authors collaborate through the publishing process, building on each other's knowledge and applying what they learn in the next phase of marketing their books. Seek out a community that isn't just led from the top down, but one that empowers and supports each member, fostering collective growth as they write.

Professional fiction author Jonathan Yanez calls his community the Pack based on the name of his company, Wolf Pack Entertainment. Whenever he posts on social media, it's always highlighting people in the Pack. He made the cover of *Indie Author Magazine,* and for the photoshoot, he turned his face to the side so the focus would be on his shirt that highlighted his Pack. In the article, he stressed the importance of every member of his community, and how he wouldn't be where he is right now without the *Pack.* Every time you talk to Jonathan, you get the sense of how important this group is to him. He never makes it about himself or the accomplishments he's made, but always redirects it to his community of readers that are amazing. His group feels seen, heard, and understood.

COMMUNITY LAUNCHPAD

Meetups

The best way you can get to know your readers is to host a meetup. When Jonathan travels and speaks in certain destinations, he now includes meetups with people in his community. His readers travel thousands of miles to come to one of these meetups. It may start out small with a few people at the beginning, but it's similar to writing your first book; it grows as you do it.

The meetups give readers a chance to get to know not only you, but also other fans in the community. This is a fantastic way to increase the bond in the community. They'll feel seen and understood, and a beautiful connection is made between everyone in the community as subgroups from the larger community begin to develop.

As you begin to grow your own community or fan base, make sure to stress how important they are to the vitality of all the books you write. Especially in this era of virtual meetings, there's nothing that compares with a personal, in person meetup.

The well-known author C.S. Lewis was a prominent member of the *Inklings*, a community of authors who knew the value of being in a writing community with other fascinating literary minds, including J.R.R. Tolkien. Some of the most renowned stories were birthed from that group that met for nearly two decades. Books like Lewis's *Chronicles of Narnia*, *The Screwtape Letters*, and *Prince Caspian*, and Tolkien's legends, *Lord of the Rings*, *The Hobbit*, and his translation of *Beowulf*. Iron sharpens iron, and these men were proof of this as they faithfully met to produce some of the most well-known epic high fantasy novels that millions of people still know and love today.

This road to writing and marketing isn't a straight line. Many authors want a checklist on how to "make it" or sell more books. But what if it's all about honing your craft, writing more than one book, so when God

LAUNCHING YOU

launches you, you hit the target with such velocity it breaks open the door of opportunity that you never saw coming? It takes *intentional time* spent with other authors to fully propel you into the destiny that God has for you.

It Takes a Team

Launching isn't a solo activity. Thousands of people worked on the Space Shuttle, yet there were only seven astronauts who launched into space. A diverse group of engineers, scientists, logisticians, and a host of others were needed to prepare and launch the spacecraft. It takes an entire team to *launch well*. Jesus called twelve to be His apostles (special messengers), but there were at least seventy others who helped launch His ministry, and then 120 in that upper room in Acts who would change the course of history. You're not meant to go alone; it will take a big investment for you to be launched. An investment in time, focus, and finances to get you to the *launch pad*, as well as a community to *propel you* into the stratosphere.

This journey will require mentors and a community you trust. Those you pour into, and those who pour into you. Then the support team will be in place to launch you to new heights.

My parents loved NASCAR. The cars would go around the track repeatedly, but at some point in the race, the driver would need to drive into the pit, and the pit crew would work on getting the car ready for the next leg of the race. Each person on the crew had a specific duty they were tasked with to get that race car back on the track to win. We all need a pit crew. Those with publishing experience, combined with the enthusiastic support of fans cheering you on like a great cloud of witnesses, will propel you forward faster and further than you could ever achieve alone. Find a community that supports you, and you'll win the race that God has specifically designed for you to win. Run in such a way to win, with your pit crew at your side.

COMMUNITY LAUNCHPAD

We're born to be in a community. At Square Tree, our writing cohorts give the encouragement authors need to keep going when, at times, they want to quit and walk away. They find the courage amongst each other to learn new business skills needed in the days to come, and the focus to stay on the course no matter what may come their way. The test of a great author community is that it promotes regular prayer, encouraging critique groups, and referential marketing, all wrapped up in a spirit of generosity to help see each other launch.

Children's author Irene Murphy recently expressed her gratitude for the support she's found in her cohort community.

"I have people now. I always wanted to have people. I found them when I joined the cohort."

Once she found her people within our Square Tree writers' cohort, she created a YouTube channel with two other members, launched her *Story Time with Oma Murphy* channel, and has just published her second children's book, with three more on the way. "I couldn't have done it without the support and prayers of my cohort."

Prayer

"It seems like all hell is breaking loose in my life since I started writing my book" is a common cry from Christian authors.

Numerous trials hit when writers put their pen to paper. I'd make a bet you have experienced this as well! Maybe the trials have even set you back months or years in your writing. Since your stories are life-changing and have the power to shift culture, change atmospheres, and help others find the breakthrough they desperately need, is it any wonder that it feels like you're in the middle of a spiritual battle? Whether it's writing fiction or nonfiction, the greater the assignment, the bigger the warfare, in order to prepare you for what is to come.

LAUNCHING YOU

Prayer is a critical piece to any healthy writer's community. Fighting the battle together through prayer brings you even closer to one another. It creates a bond in the trenches as you're writing your books. God says to pick up your sword and fight, and the sword for an author is their pen. You need to keep writing even through the warfare.

Consistently praying and sharing with other authors is critical as you write your book, and for some, it can literally save their life.

One of our authors faithfully showed up to her writers' cohort group even while she was recovering from major surgery in the hospital! It was that connection and feeling of a greater purpose with like-minded, praying people that gave her hope in the often-hopeless situation she faced. That is the power of these intimate writers' cohorts. The enemy's attacks can be strong, but together we are stronger.

Draft off One Another

I love to wake up on Saturday mornings to ride my bike on the beach trails in Southern California. One weekend, I jumped on my bicycle and was riding at a steady pace, with the wind behind my back, pressing me forward. I thought I was going fast, until I kept seeing groups of bikers going twice as fast and blowing right past me.

The riders formed a line, staying as close as they could to the front rider. This is called *drafting*. It creates a low-pressure area behind you, reducing wind resistance. You can then pedal at the same speed, but with less effort. The second rider in this draft can save as much as *40% of their energy* just by trailing the leader, and drafting even helps the leader, allowing them to conserve 4% of their energy.

Being in a community as you're *drafting your manuscript* is important and will help pull you forward, even on your hardest days. It is harder alone. You know this. Accountability, encouragement, and those who will

COMMUNITY LAUNCHPAD

help you through all the resistance are invaluable. You need the support of a group of writers so you can make tremendous progress and accelerate the time it takes you to finish your book.

You Need an Accelerant

"Do you want to take the FasTrak?" I felt in my spirit one day, as I was driving on the freeway.

It was my eighth year in business, and I was frustrated. While working late nights to serve my authors and feeling like I'd failed more times than I succeeded, I saw a Facebook ad for a challenge and decided to join to get more ideas for the company. Julie Chenell spoke at the event, and I loved her honesty, transparency, and intelligence. She was clearly well beyond my own business acumen in terms of running an online business. I really wanted to join her business mentoring group, Digital Insiders, but when I found out how much it cost, I balked.

"God, I really want to join this mastermind group, but it's a lot of money…should I join?" I kept asking while deep in thought as I drove.

Distracted, I ended up missing the onramp to the FasTrak lane. FasTrak allows you to drive in a special paid lane on the highway, bypassing heavy traffic. Stressed that I missed my opportunity and was now sitting in a ton of traffic, I inched my way until I got another opportunity to get back into the FasTrak lane.

It was then I heard God clearly say, "Joining the FasTrak lane is like joining Digital Insiders. You can either sit in traffic and wait for a long time, or invest some money with this mentor, and get there faster. Either way, you'll get there, but the choice is yours."

It was such a physical example of how stepping out in faith financially to invest in yourself moves you to your destination faster.

LAUNCHING YOU

It's not about the money; it's about the mentor and the community. That day on the freeway is forever etched in my memory as I said "yes" to God and joined Digital Insiders.[1]

I wasn't sure how I was going to pay for the bill each month, but God has provided every year I've been in this mastermind program. It wasn't some big miraculous provision that came, but a steady amount of income that allowed me to continue in the group. And Square Tree Publishing has grown more in the past three years than in the previous eight years combined. But it took me saying YES to a seemingly impossible financial investment to see God's miraculous provision and the growth of the company each month.

It has been the BEST decision I've made in years!

I joined the group because Julie is amazing, but the gold is also among the people in the group that she's curated. DI gave me a sense of community; I was not alone and could ask them for advice or support anytime I needed it. The adage *"you don't know what you don't know"* was true in this situation. I didn't know a mentor and a community were exactly what I needed, but God did.

It takes courage to give God your YES when you have absolutely no idea what lies ahead or how the finances will come in. Honestly, I have seen more financial miracles in our author community than I can count, and surprisingly, it coincided with God testing my own faith financially. Authors who were on disability, retired, or single moms scraping to get by, gave God their YES and saw the Heavens opened, seas parted, and the funding to make their God-sized dream come from unexpected places.

Square Tree author Louann was obedient when the Holy Spirit spoke to her about quitting her job. It was a tough decision, but she found the courage to do it in faith to write her book. After she quit, she randomly

---

[1] https://digitalinsidersmastermind.co/intro?am_id=sherry

COMMUNITY LAUNCHPAD

cleaned her bathroom closet and found an eyeglass case. She opened the case and found over $4,000, and then an additional $100 in a spare purse. She has no recollection of ever putting any of it there.

One Square Tree author had forgiven a past abuser who ended up giving her the exact amount she needed to pay for her publishing. Another Square Tree author and her husband wrote out all the financial miracles on a yellow legal pad, and there were over two double-sided pages of provision. It all came from various places from sudden discounts, generous gifts, return of overpayments, refunds, and the list goes on. But there were more blessings than just financial. God blessed them with the increase in leveling up in other areas God wanted to give them. They sold their house, reconnected with best friends in a new community, received promises directly from God, made great new friends, and she wrote five more books in her series. In addition, her lifelong prayer came to fruition when she hugged her birth mother for the very first time in thirty-six years.

Many have found surprise checks in the mail or been blessed by sudden generosity from loved ones supporting them in their dream to become an author. So many stories I don't have space to tell, but…

It only came AFTER they gave God their yes. Only after they proved their faith by taking that first scary step of obedience. Only after they walked away from distractions and excuses and leaned into what God was doing.

As you begin to walk in obedience to become an author and steward what God has called you to do, doors will open that you never dreamed would open, bringing some of the most wonderful surprises of your life!

Plus, you'll get the extra bonus of doing all of this within a community of like-minded believers cheering you on as you become a published author, all while improving your writing skills.

LAUNCHING YOU

Cohort (Critique) Groups

While it's equally important to make sure your writing group is highly encouraging, it is crucial they provide honest and supportive feedback about the edits you'll need to make to improve your book.

Friends and family will usually encourage you, but honest feedback is invaluable. A professional writing coach is necessary to increase your writing skills and to make your manuscript as clean as possible. First impressions are tremendously important, and being in a cohort helps you see how people respond immediately as you read parts of your book to them. Feedback can make or break your message.

It's normal to be fearful at first. You may be unsure how other authors will respond to your book, but the longer you're in the group, the more you begin to desire this feedback and look forward to sharing what you've written. The fear will leave, and your confidence will grow exponentially.

Your cohort members become trusted friends and will promote your book once the book is published. It's like having an entire marketing team making connections for you, the "rocket accelerant" you'll need to launch the message you are carrying.

Marketing Together

"I talked to the manager of a local bookstore who's reserving an entire bookshelf for any of the Square Tree authors in our community," Lynn told her writers' cohort.

Lynn began networking with a bookstore owner, not just for her own book but for all the other authors in her writers' group (and she hasn't even finished her own book yet!). Marlena has begun to bundle all the children's books from her cohort group into a beautiful package for baby showers to spread the word about her cohort members who have published.

COMMUNITY LAUNCHPAD

That is the power of being not only in community, but the *right* community. One where everyone has a seat at the table and each author in the group is doing their part to give one another a leg up in spreading the word about each other's book. These types of communities reap an entire grassroots marketing team who are constantly looking for marketing opportunities to promote both their books and other authors' books. It shifts the thinking from "I gotta get my book out" to "Let's get everyone's book on that same bookshelf."

Generosity Reigns

You want to pick a community where generosity is evident in all they do. In our community, the motto is "All boats float," meaning everyone helps one another with what they need so all may prosper. Our community has given to date: multiple laptop computers to authors who needed them; donated dozens of tickets to authors to attend our writing events; gifted courses to writers; and enabled others to attend cohorts for a time, for free. It has produced a spirit of generosity, which has become contagious. Everyone is excited to cheer each other on toward publishing and to help equip one another with the tools they need to finish their books.

It truly is more blessed to give than to receive. And as you pour into your local community of authors, you'll feel the love and generosity flow back to you.

LAUNCHING YOU

 Pro Tip:
Be obedient to what God is telling you to do even if it makes no sense and your bank account disagrees! You just don't know what is on the other side of giving God your YES.

 Launching YOU Into Action
1. Ask God which author community is right for you and your book. Then join the group even if it costs you in time and finances.
2. Join a Writers' Cohort or critique group so you can get better as a writer. Steward what God has given you.
3. Just as one spacecraft's mission can catapult another, what are two ways you can help support another author today?

CHAPTER 12
LAUNCHING A MOVEMENT

On May 25, 1961, President Kennedy, amidst the backdrop of the cold war with Russia, gave a speech to the special joint session of Congress.

"I believe we should go to the Moon. Let it be clear...that I'm asking the Congress and the country to accept a firm commitment to a new course of action...a course which will last for many years and carry a very heavy cost: $531 million dollars...an estimated $7-$9 billion dollars additional over the next five years. If we're to go only halfway, or reduce our sights in the face of difficulty, in my judgment, it would be better not to go at all." Congress agreed with President Kennedy, and the space movement began.[1]

The dream came true eight years later, on July 20, 1969, as Neil Armstrong and Edwin (Buzz) Aldrin, in their Lunar Module Eagle, landed on the Moon. Armstrong, confirming the landing, said to Duke at NASA, "Houston, Tranquility Base here." He then uttered the well-known phrase, "The Eagle has landed."[2]

---

[1] The Decision to Go to the Moon: President John F. Kennedy's May 25, 1961 Speech before a Joint Session of Congress - NASA

[2] 50 Years Ago: One Small Step, One Giant Leap - NASA

LAUNCHING YOU

As Armstrong got out of the Eagle and stepped foot on the Moon, he spoke those famous words, "That's one small step for man, one giant leap for mankind." What isn't as well-known is that right before Aldrin got out of Eagle, he made a request: "I'd like to take this opportunity to ask every person listening in, whoever and wherever they may be, to pause for a moment and contemplate the events of the past few hours and to give thanks in his or her own way." He then proceeded to take communion before he stepped out on the Moon.

****

A movement is a heavy assignment from God. It's not to be taken lightly. It will last for many years and carry a heavy cost that you'll pay spiritually. As Aldrin gave thanks and took communion, putting God first, so too God MUST be at the forefront of any movement. If you start a movement, it will be up to *you* to sustain that movement for years to come. You may end up only going halfway or reducing your sights in the face of difficulty.

However, if God builds the movement, it will be His to sustain. If God is asking you to start a movement, then know there will be a spiritual price tag attached to His calling. You may face warfare in the form of resistance or trials, or it may take years to reach the point of launching—and the finances needed to sustain it.

So, count the cost and consciously give God your YES, knowing that He'll sustain you through the ups and downs that will certainly come with that assignment. The movement may be greater than what you see now.

Science Behind It Movement

At the tender age of nine, Zandra Cunningham's dad said he wouldn't buy her any more lip gloss, so she took it upon herself to learn how to create it in the kitchen from natural plants. Now, at twenty-three years old, she

LAUNCHING A MOVEMENT

runs a national skincare line called Zandra Beauty, and the brand is all about elevating girls and women. It was tough to find people who would take her seriously at such a young age, but now, with a thriving business, charity foundation, book, and potential reality TV show, she's found much success.

In addition to all this success, she's creating a movement within her business. It was not something she planned, but God opened doors for Zandra to create the Science Behind It Movement. At the beginning, it was about creating workshops to help other young people learn how to make different types of skin products and to show them the possibility of starting their own businesses at a young age. It morphed from how to formulate products into learning about the business side of those products.

Zandra didn't wake up one day and say, "I want to create a movement." It happened as she gave God her yes, and the doors of opportunity swung wide open to her and her family. Her focus was on helping and empowering young girls, which in turn launched a movement. She wanted to create impact by shifting the lives of young people, helping them accomplish more, and elevating them to new levels in business.

Zandra's mom, Tamara, created a new business called Raising a Mogul through supporting her daughter. Her business helps other parents with young children who want to create a business and supports them through that process. She expressed how important your WHY must be, and the WHO you're doing it for, especially with the cutthroat competitive market.

"When you're so focused on the people you're determined to impact and help with your own mission, then anyone coming to copycat what you're doing won't matter anymore. When you remember you're doing it for the 'one,' then it brings you back into alignment."

When you become a pioneer, there will be people who come alongside and try to "knock off" what you're doing, stealing from what you've built. But because you have paid a price to get where you are and have the rock-

LAUNCHING YOU

solid inner knowing of your why and who you're serving, no one will be able to steal anything from what you have created.

"Many movements you have heard about have longevity and can live on for years to come. What messaging and goal do you want to carry out in your movement that will impact the next generation?" Zandra explained.

"The movement is bigger than us. Even if your why is huge and massive, if you get caught up in the day-to-day and focus only on what is happening at this moment, there will be so many things to block you from moving forward. You need to remember it's bigger than you. It's going to be hard with many people who don't believe in you, so you need to be on your knees with God so that you're ready."

Building a movement creates an impact and changes lives, and it will naturally transform your own life as well. Take the focus off yourself and put it on the experience of serving the world and the people you want to help, and it can't help but impact you in the most positive ways.

There are a multitude of ways to build a movement and many more ways to make an impact. Whether it be in business or ministry, movements are a powerful way to create impact and leave a legacy for the next generation. Borrowing the phrase from Neil Armstrong, this could be one of those "small steps for man, giant leap for mankind" moments to look back on.

Flagship Company

Last year, our Square Tree intercessory team came to me with a prophetic word over the company.

"Square Tree is an aircraft carrier, and it was carrying two flags; it had support ships flanking it."

One of the flags was white, symbolizing peace, and the other flag was a medical flag, symbolizing healing. The support ships flanking it were our intercessory prayer team, and I'm sure other ministries will be revealed as we

LAUNCHING A MOVEMENT

keep going. Years earlier, I had been given a prophetic word from one of our authors that we were a flagship business. When I studied aircraft carriers, I was shocked to see that it's a modern-day battleship, and it's also a *flagship*.

I was stunned.

The more I began to research it and pray, the more the meaning revealed itself. Square Tree is a launching pad for authors. Just like an aircraft carrier launching many different types of planes and helicopters, so too will Square Tree launch many different types of authors.

An aircraft carrier is surrounded by many offensive battleships to keep the ship safe. Our intercessors told us that we would need an even bigger prayer team to cover us as we move forward.

A bigger prayer fleet to launch authors like you! Authors who will shape culture and shift atmospheres. Authors who will launch internationally, transforming nations. Authors will be firestarters, launching multiple movements!

555 Movement

"I need us to go to Taiwan," Melodie Fox, our Square Tree editor, said to me one day. She was working on the story of human trafficking survivor Shari Ho who was sold as a slave in Taiwan and brought to the United States. As we prepared to go, I kept seeing the number 555 all around me. It would pop up on my phone, or I'd see it on a huge billboard when I was driving down the freeway, or when I looked at the clock in the kitchen. Everywhere I looked, that number was highlighted to me. I asked God one day what it meant, and He gave me the Scripture Isaiah 55:5.

"Surely you will summon nations you know not, and nations you do not know will come running to you, because of the Lord your God, the Holy One of Israel, for he has endowed you with splendor."[1]

---

[1] Isaiah 55:5 (NIV)

LAUNCHING YOU

During that time, we helped launch three different authors into their ministries. We had a special scripture for each ministry. All three verses ended the exact same way: because He has endowed you with splendor.

In Hebrew, each letter also represents a number and a picture. The word splendor means, "Because you humbled yourself and spoke with the Father first, He'll glorify you and He'll be glorified."

The Hebrew number for splendor is eighty. Moses was eighty years old when he led the people in a mass exodus out of slavery. When you read this same word represented by the numbers, it means, "Because you spoke with the Father and asked, there will be a great exodus for a new beginning for many."

This is exactly what we're praying and believing for through Shari Ho's story. Our prayer is there will be a great exodus and a new beginning for many victims of human trafficking.

Several months later, we flew to Taiwan and arrived at our Airbnb, which was in the heart of the night market. At three in the morning, God woke me up and said, "Put on your shoes, walk the land, and start declaring Isaiah 55:5 over the nation."

I put my slippers on and began to pace back and forth in the room I was staying in, declaring that verse. The rest of the trip was amazing! We signed contracts with a Taiwanese Christian publisher, Elim Publishing.

Several years later, we met an amazing Taiwanese family living in the United States. They came onboard as strategic partners to help get Shari's book, which had been translated into Mandarin Chinese, out to the Taiwanese churches.

They mentioned this movement they had been part of called Taiwan for Jesus 555. Jane Buscemi from Blazing Glories Ministries partnered with Dr. Joseph Nassralla to be part of this movement.

"Why is the movement called 555?" I excitedly asked Jane in one of our meetings.

LAUNCHING A MOVEMENT

"Because the movement was based on Isaiah 55:5," she stated, matter-of-factly.

I was shocked when she said this. As we continued to talk and I did the math in my head, we both realized that we had been in Taiwan the same year and at the same time when God woke me up at 3 A.M. to pray Isaiah 55:5 over the land! This was no coincidence; God was up to something big in Taiwan.

This movement was about unifying the Christian churches, helping them go beyond the four walls of the church to declare Taiwan as a land for Jesus. Each of the churches would have members hold flags and go outside and walk the city together with the other churches to show solidarity. This movement lasted four years, but I believe it's only the beginning. God is getting ready to move again in the nation of Taiwan. There's a second wave of the movement coming to Taiwan, and it will be on the heels of Shari Ho's story.

For some of you, God wants to create a movement through your stories, books, or business. It may start out small and grow progressively, or it may just explode onto the scene. Or it may be a movement that has already started, which you'll partner with to fuel the fire and birth another, bigger movement. Know that what you do in private as you humble yourself in the secret place will decide the trajectory of the path God has for you and your book, for He has endowed you with splendor to create a movement.

When we began the journey with Shari's story, we had no idea if it would turn into a movement someday. It was just a faithful walk, only doing the next step He told us to do along the way. The journey has been fraught with a lot of peaks and valleys, but the bigger the assignment, the more that comes against you, so prepare yourself in that secret place and God will sustain you through it all. In the words of former President Kennedy, *"If*

LAUNCHING YOU

you're to go only halfway, or reduce your sights in the face of difficulty, in my judgment, it would be better not to go at all." There will be a steep price to pay in creating a movement, so get grounded before it launches.

It's also important to build a prayer team to support you so you're not alone. As we're growing, we're realizing that we now need a bigger prayer team to support the work that God is about to do. Select a prayer team that is faithfully praying for you on a regular basis and can share what they feel God is impressing upon them. This will help confirm some of the ideas God is downloading to you and give you direction for the future God has for you as you pray into it.

Stay open to how God wants to launch you and use your book. It just may look like a movement!

 **Pro Tip:**

If God wants to start a movement, count the cost before you give God your yes. But when you say yes, set your face like flint toward it and don't look back no matter the cost.

Launch YOU Into Action

1. Pray to God and see if there's any place in your heart where you have not put Him first in your life. Repent because He's the one who must lead the movement, not you.
2. The key to any movement is to serve others. What ways can you serve your current audience to steward what you currently have?
3. If you're starting a movement, having a consistent prayer intercessory team is essential. (I believe in blessing your prayer team financially each month.) Who is God calling you to partner with as a prayer team?

CONCLUSION
REENTRY

I watched in disbelief in this déjà vu moment as an explosive fire trail began to streak across the sky, breaking apart the reentry of the Space Shuttle Columbia and killing all seven crew members. Its debris fell from the atmosphere from California all the way to Texas.

On takeoff, seven million pounds of thrust launched the shuttle into orbit. The Columbia launch seemed successful as the astronauts circled Earth for sixteen days.

But what they didn't realize was a piece of foam insulation, the size of a briefcase, broke off the shuttle's propellant tank during the launch and damaged the left wing of the plane and the heat-resistant tiles.

NASA knew similar incidents had occurred on three prior shuttle launches without causing critical impairment, yet they chose not to address the matter. The heat shield tiles were a recurring issue in the design of the Space Shuttle, constantly being damaged and replaced. Damage to tiles in the upper portion of the shuttle was less critical compared to damage in the middle underbelly. The Columbia's compromised tiles were located near the landing gear and key electronic systems essential for flying the shuttle.[1]

---

[1] Space Shuttle Columbia Disaster - Cause, Crew & Impact | HISTORY

LAUNCHING YOU

This accident could have been prevented by moving up the planned Atlantis launch date to either repair the wing or get the crew off the Columbia. However, NASA never notified the astronauts of the situation. The compression shock wave hit the shuttle as it entered the Earth's atmosphere, and fire encompassed the vehicle as it was going 12,500 miles per hour. The heat shields were their only means of defense against the 1,600 Celsius temperatures upon reentry, and the "wind and heat entered the damaged wing, damaging the hydraulic systems and sending the shuttle into an unrecoverable spin that caused it to break apart." The astronauts were fitted with parachutes in an emergency, but they had to wait until they were past this shock wave process of reentry.

What didn't kill them when they were launched, killed them upon reentry. Liftoff and reentry are the most dangerous times to be on a rocket, with so much explosive energy that can go violently wrong. One small, yet significant accident blew up and incinerated the entire mission, and the astronauts didn't know about it until reentry.

****

God has a mission for you. He wants to prepare you for launch and is concerned about even the smallest details in your situation, which may seem inconsequential to you. God knows if He launches you too soon in the wrong conditions, you'll blow up and self-destruct like the *Challenger* did. But He also knows that even if you are launched successfully, even a small issue (the size of a briefcase), can take you out upon reentry.

Jared, Commander of Inspiration4, said, "You don't know if you took a hit, until you hit the Earth's atmosphere (on reentry)."

God knows if you took that hit as you launched, so trust Him with the timing of your reentry.

Reentry is what happens *after* the launch. After all your friends and

CONCLUSION

family have bought your book, it can get quiet. Breaking off limiting beliefs during reentry is a necessary part of the process. Don't despise those days. God is still fully developing you so you don't self-destruct in the next step He has for you. God is giving you the grit to handle the next phase of the launch.

When Joseph, in the Bible, was promoted to head servant in Potiphar's house, he was launched into his new position and carried a tremendous amount of authority. However, he was falsely accused and thrown in jail. After interpreting the cupbearer and the baker's dreams, the cupbearer reneged on his promise to help free him. Joseph sat in prison for two more years until he was launched into his true destiny. It was in those two years when "life doesn't make sense" that a person's character is tested. Stay the course. Joseph ended up in the highest position, with the most influence, to the greatest Pharaoh in the known world! Joseph gained authority, power, and influence and was on a God-mission to save the whole world. But God knew the right moment and conditions for this to take place.

Be open to what reentry looks like for you. God knows where you have been and where you're going, even if it doesn't make sense. Make sure to follow His lead during this time so your reentry goes as planned.

Misfire Reentry

It was years of work culminating in a single day...a single launch. When human trafficking survivor Shari Ho was freed after twenty years, CNN ran a story about her, which kicked off a media firestorm. The Taiwanese government stepped in to pay for her trip to Taiwan to locate and reunite her with her family. She instantly became famous overnight, and even bodyguards were hired to protect her from the crowds and media that mobbed her.

LAUNCHING YOU

When we launched her book, *My Name Is Also Freedom*, we thought the same media attention would happen again. We decided to create an entire event around human trafficking awareness and invited all the local nonprofits in the area to be part of it. We created a buzz! Over thirty-five vendors were invited, along with radio interviews, and even a local senator.

We brought in local talent and made it all about arts and entertainment with dancers, spoken word poetry, and an artist painting to music. It took months of planning with an entire team to coordinate the performances and speakers. Nearly 400 attended the event. But eight days prior, everything seemed to fall apart when those who had promised to host the venue "for free" charged us thousands of dollars. It was too late to back out because we had already sold hundreds of tickets. In the end, we were lucky to break even. Shari thought her entire life was going to change; she'd finally have money, and her phone would be ringing with numerous offers for speaking engagements.

Then reentry came.

Only a few speaking engagements materialized, and Shari's life went back to normal. It was a huge blow not only to Shari but to our entire team as well.

But her story isn't over yet. Fast forward six years: her book has been translated into Mandarin, and we're ready for a book launch in Taiwan. The media has already been asking for interviews, and God has put in my spirit that something big is about to happen. I wish I could say it has been smooth sailing *this* time, but there still have been hurdles to jump over and bumps in the road that need navigating, but that moment WILL come. Why didn't it happen six years ago? God only knows. But I do believe He still needed to prepare not only Shari Ho, but also our entire team to go back to Taiwan. Like Joseph, who spent two more years in jail and was seemingly forgotten, it was only part of his story.

CONCLUSION

The "hit" we took to our wings during the first launch has since been resolved. The key is to trust God in what happens next so there will be no self-implosion during reentry.

Fast Reentry

Anthony Brown experienced a huge media response when his book, *From Park Bench to Park Avenue: One Man's Journey Out of Homelessness*, was published. He's been on several media outlets, including the Dr. Drew Show, and has spoken several times about legislation for homelessness in California. Additionally, he is on the board of the Schizophrenia and Psychosis Action Alliance. Square Tree Productions is now working on turning his story into a movie! His reentry was more than he ever could have imagined, and he's taking off like a rocket.

Steady Reentry

After Cathy Taylor's curriculum, *Hurting Moms, Mending Hearts,* was published, it began to grow steadily for the first four years and ended up getting over five million views on her Facebook page. She's set up support groups in churches all over the United States and Canada. Her journey was not an overnight success, but a slow and steady climb to where she now has over 100,000 followers on Facebook. Her reentry was years in the making, steadily increasing each year.

Reentry Into a Business

When I wrote my book, *Wilderness Season*, it helped launch a brand-new business, Square Tree Publishing. I didn't even have it on my radar, and yet God opened doors to start a publishing company, which has now grown into a production company, Square Tree Productions, with two sci-fi movies heading toward streaming services. I was obedient to write

LAUNCHING YOU

the book God asked me to, and then business doors began to open. It has taken over a decade to get to this place, with mistakes littered in the hallways of obedience, but it has truly been worth the wait.

Dr. Amanda Helman's book, *Silenced No Longer*, helped her birth a coaching business, and she's become the Square Tree Cognitive Release Coach for our authors. Her book broke the silence in her own life and created a brand-new business for her in the field of speaking and coaching. Her breakthrough had the extra benefit of having her join the Square Tree team and help thousands of authors find their own voice in the journey of writing their books.

Transforming Reentry

We have also seen many authors whose lives returned to "normal," where the media storm *didn't* hit, and thousands of books were not sold. But they were transformed. They were forever changed. There's no price you can put on a Spiritual ROI (Return on Investment). And for some authors, the difference was so amazing, they were unrecognizable after they had published. They had incredible breakthroughs in their lives personally, and had finally found their voice that had been silenced for years.

Purpose of Reentry

The crux in reentry: What is God's goal for having you write the book? Was it mostly for healing? Was it to build your business or to become a speaker? Was it to birth a ministry? Your reentry will line up with God's objective. For some of you, it will be like a rocket that never lands, and you'll just keep soaring; for others, it will be a steady, slow climb upward to amazing heights. But for those of you who may feel you got the consolation prize of "only" receiving a personal breakthrough, know it will be like one you've never seen before, which will, in turn,

CONCLUSION

open new doors for you that you never knew were there.

Trust God no matter what happens in reentry, knowing that He's got you and still has a great plan for your life. Knowing your WHY in writing the book will help ground you during reentry and allow you to have peace no matter what happens. Reentry is never unfruitful with God at the helm.

Do you trust God through this process?

If so, then get grounded and stay the course, for you never know what is on the other side of your yes to Him, even after reentry.

 Pro Tip:

Trust God no matter what your reentry looks like, and keep listening for His next set of instructions. Then, in simple obedience, do it.

 Launching YOU Into Action

1. Check in with God WHY you are writing the book. It will ground you when you come into reentry, no matter which way it goes.
2. Ask God what area He still needs to work on in you so you don't implode after you have launched.
3. Write down some people you could contact to speak or become a guest on a podcast to keep the momentum going after you launch.

NOT YOUR TYPICAL EPILOGUE
IT'S NOT ABOUT YOU!

"I just want to throw in the towel on this business!" I said one day after a grueling week running my publishing company.

"Take that towel, get on your knees, and begin to use it to wash the feet of those authors that you serve," God instructed.

I wasn't expecting that.

I wanted to be coddled and told that everything was going to be okay, and that all the hard trials I was going through would be resolved.

That's not what I got from the Lord.

I got a lesson in servanthood with the "towel" of a business He's given to me.

This whole book has been about launching YOU.

But what if it's *not about you* as much as it's about being obedient to *Him* and serving those around you?

I felt impressed to write a book about launching you a year ago, and God was relentless, making sure I knew how important this book was to Him. He stressed that I needed to complete the book within months and not to delay in writing it. I was excited yet confused about what I was going to write.

God said, "The revelations will come in the writing."

A few weeks later, I went to King Camp through Bear Creek Ministries for deep inner healing. The bottom line I walked away with that weekend was…

LAUNCHING YOU

It's NOT about you!

How in the world was I going to hold these two different words I had from the Lord in tension?

God wanting to launch you, but it's _not_ about you.

God wants to (and will) launch you, but the *launch isn't the focus.* Our affection, devotion, and attention need to be on Jesus. As we lay down all our dreams, desires, and decisions at His feet, we need to completely surrender our will for His. The litmus test is knowing that if God asked us to walk away from all of it, at any time, anywhere in the process…we would.

But not walking away in an "I'm not worthy" wrong mindset kind of way, but walking away even in confidence.

Therein lies the tension. The tension between co-partnering with God and knowing that He really doesn't need you. The tension between launching you, but it's not about you. Staying low, so He can raise you up and launch you at the proper time.

I hope this book has shown you the endless possibilities for authors just like yourself, and how God used their books to launch them. Most didn't even know the *doors of opportunity* that would meet them in the *hallways of obedience.* But their focus was not on the doors, but in the hallways of the unknown, willing to obey God no matter what.

"Are you willing to pay the price for what I'm about to give you?" God asked me one day in prayer.

I struggled with the answer, thinking everything was a free gift from God.

"Yes, no matter what," I finally said.

"No matter what?" He questioned.

"No matter what," I said, not knowing what was about to come to me.

Over a decade followed in a "Wilderness" season, and it was filled

EPILOGUE

with tremendous trials and heartaches, but the richness that deepened my relationship with God…I wouldn't trade for anything in the world. I couldn't have said that even a few years ago, but looking back, it's what brought me to my knees, continually humbled and knowing I couldn't do anything except by Him.

As you're in the *hallways of obedience* writing your book, dig deeper into God than you ever have before.

Will you get launched after you write the book?

Probably.

But, *by then it won't even matter.*

You'll be launched into a deeper relationship with Him.

Therein lies the deeper revelation.

Then the doors of opportunities are limitless!

A GIFT FOR YOU

You've just unlocked your bonuses to help propel not only your book, but everything that needs to come into alignment for your launch.

Grab your insider tips, exclusive workshops, and behind-the-scenes secrets to launch not only your book but YOU!

Get your bonuses now at **www.launchingauthors.com/bonuses.**

ABOUT THE AUTHOR

From appearing on national TV to inspiring movements and building businesses, Sherry Ward's mission is all about launching people beyond their books—empowering them to make a difference in ways they never imagined. As the CEO of Square Tree Publishing & Productions and founder of Christian Creators 360, Sherry brings over a decade of expertise in transforming aspiring authors into bold, purpose-driven voices. Known for her appearance on Good Morning America and her work as an executive producer for two sci-fi thrillers, she skillfully blends industry savvy with heartfelt connection. Outside of work, Sherry opens her home to young adults, offering encouragement, mentorship, and the reminder that every story matters.

Contact: info@squaretreepublishing.com
Facebook: https://www.facebook.com/squaretreepublishing
Instagram: https://www.instagram.com/squaretreepublishing/
LinkedIn: https://www.linkedin.com/in/sherrylynnward/
YouTube: https://www.youtube.com/@squaretreepublishing3278

SPEAKER PAGE

Sherry Ward is an author, speaker, and mentor who transforms aspiring authors' "little book projects" into big opportunities. With a unique blend of faith, creativity, and practical advice, she shows writers how to create books that build stages, attract clients, and leave lasting legacies.

Sherry's engaging masterclasses and keynotes inspire audiences to turn their ideas into stories so powerful, even online trolls want a signed copy. Invite Sherry to speak and watch your audience unlock their potential—one page at a time.

Topics Sherry Covers:
- God's Turning Your 'Little Book Project' Into a Full-Blown Life Catapult!
- Books Don't Sit on Shelves: They Open Stages, Attract Clients, and Build Legacies
- Write a Book So Good Even Online Trolls Ask for a Signed Copy

To book Sherry as a speaker for your next event, contact us at: www.launchingauthors.com/speaking

ALSO BY SHERRY WARD

ACKNOWLEDGEMENTS

Thank you to my incredible Square Tree Publishing team for your unwavering dedication, compassionate hearts, and steadfast devotion to our authors. I've kissed a lot of frogs to find you, but there's no one else I'd rather do life and business with. May you all be launched both personally and professionally, and see all your dreams come true in this new season.

RESOURCES

Ready to blast off on your writing adventure?

Our resource page has everything you need to rocket your book to the next level!

Visit now to unlock your writer's block, avoid common writing meltdowns, and even discover the secret formula for turning your book into a bestseller!

Don't miss out—because who wouldn't want their book to be an unputdownable favorite?

Resources Include:
- Writing Coach – Private or Group
- Exclusive Workshops and Trainings
- Writing Tools and Templates
- Author Marketing
- Writer's Tracking System
- Publishing Services

Head to **www.launchingauthors.com/resources** now and kickstart your writing adventure!

If you enjoyed this book, I'd be so grateful if you'd WRITE A REVIEW….

It's easy and helps my book get into the hands of more readers.
- Step 1: Go to www.AMAZON.com
- Step 2: Search for my book in Amazon books
- Step 3: Scroll down to REVIEWS
- Step 4: Leave a Review

I'd love to know your thoughts about my book. Contact me and let me know what you got out of the book.

Thank you for your support.

At Square Tree Publishing, we believe your message matters. That is why our dedicated team of professionals is committed to bringing your literary texts and targeted curriculum to a global marketplace. We strive to make that message of the highest quality, while still maintaining your voice.

We believe in you, therefore, we provide a platform through website design, blogs, and social media campaigns to showcase your unique message. Our innovative team offers a full range of services from editing to graphic design inspired with an eye for excellence, so that your message is clearly and distinctly heard.

Whether you are a new writer needing guidance with each step of the process, or a seasoned writer, we will propel you to the next level of your development.

At Square Tree Publishing, it's all about launching YOU!

Apply TODAY to become a Square Tree author.
Go to www.squaretreepublishing.com
Click the APPLY NOW button.

www.ingramcontent.com/pod-product-compliance
Lightning Source LLC
Chambersburg PA
CBHW050257010526
44107CB00033B/1407/J